Index

See Basic Instructions for Cutting, Sewing, Appliqué, Layering, Quilting and Binding on pages 74 - 79.

 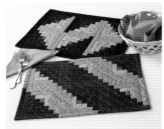

'Ott-Lite' Carry Case

Travel to your next quilt class in style and show off your love of strip piecing with the Ott-Lite Carry Case. The happy colors will draw compliments from all your friends.

continued on pages 22 - 23

'Cozy' Boxes

Organize your sewing space with Cozy Boxes that beautify your table. These soft boxes are also wonderful for a dressing table or living room shelf. Make them in your favorite fabrics to match your décor.

January

continued on pages 24 - 25

'Hugs and Kisses'

Hearts in Valentine shades of passionate pinks and reds express loving sentiments with Hugs and Kisses. Celebrate anniversaries and enchanted evenings with creative strip piecing. Hugs and Kisses makes a great table runner or wall hanging. Use the heart section on a set of place mats for a romantic dinner for two.

continued on pages 26 - 31

February

'Birds in the Air'
Wall Hanging or Table Topper

Quilters and non-sewers alike will flock to 'Birds in the Air' to examine the intricate design executed with fabulous strips and wonderful fabric placement. This project is too beautiful to put off doing and you will be proud to claim it as your own.

March

continued on pages 32 - 36

'Happy' Apron

This apron will have you seeking excuses to wear it! Bright colors and fun prints make whatever you are doing more fun.

continued on pages 37 - 41

April

May

'Batik Beauties'

Simply stunning! Dimensional flowers fill a basket with gorgeous texture and shades. Soft pastels bring flowers to life with nature's own Springtime palette.

continued on pages 42 - 47

'Jelly Roll' Pincushion

designed by Donna Thomason

What a fun way to use up some little strips and keep track of your pins at the same time. The 'Jelly Roll' pincushion is easy and quick to make. Next time you clean off your sewing table, gather up the little scraps and make a few delightful pincushions for your sewing friends.

Materials

10 strips 2" x 42"

Rubber band

24" of ribbon

Instructions

Stack the strips and roll tightly. Secure with a rubber band and tie with a ribbon.

'Jelly Roll' Pins

Quilters are always looking for fun ways to exhibit their love of quilting. 'Jelly Roll' pins are made and exchanged to celebrate workshops, retreats and gatherings.

Make one of these clever little rolls of strips at your next sewing bee or as a gift for your favorite friend.

Materials

5 strips 2½" x 20"

Rubber band

12" of ribbon

Pin back

Instructions

Fold 5 strips 2½" x 20" in half lengthwise.

Stack and roll tightly.

Secure with a rubber band and tie with a ribbon.

Sew a pin back in place.

Watermelon Place Mat

Celebrate the tastes of Summer with a set of place mats that add zest to your picnic table or breakfast nook. These Watermelon Place Mats are quick to make and fun to do. What a great gift for a summer housewarming, wedding, or birthday.

continued on pages 48 - 49

June

'Hooray'
Wall Hanging and Place Mats

Hip, Hip, Hooray! Express your patriotism with a splash of red, white, and blue on your wall or luncheon table. The place mats are made from the same block as the wall hanging. Applique a white star on a red napkin for a beautiful finish.

continued on pages 50 - 55

July

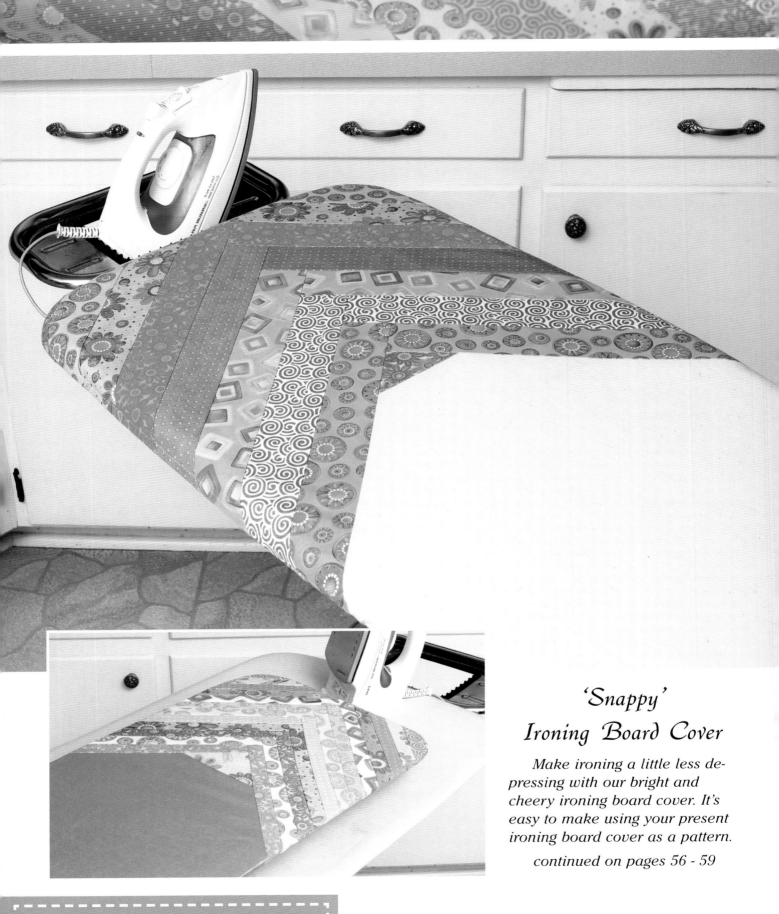

'Snappy' Ironing Board Cover

Make ironing a little less depressing with our bright and cheery ironing board cover. It's easy to make using your present ironing board cover as a pattern.

continued on pages 56 - 59

August

'Posy' Place Mat and Leaf Coaster

Looking for an alternative to the usual turkey motif for Fall? Check out this Leaf Coaster and make a bunch for your Thanksgiving gathering.

If you have wanted to try foundation piecing, here is your chance. Small projects are perfect for beginners and this one is particularly simple to execute. Be warned! Foundation piecing is addictive! This is a really fun project that is easily adapted to any décor by simply changing the colors.

continued on pages 60 - 63

September

Pumpkins Table Topper

With Jack-o-Lantern grins, these pumpkins are sure to scare up some smiles at your Halloween party. If you prefer a harvest theme, simply delete the faces from your sewing plan.

continued on pages 64 - 70

'Log Cabin' Place Mats

Recall the struggles of the pioneers as you bedeck your Thanksgiving table with Log Cabin place mats. Rotate the blocks to create a fun variety of patterns that would have been readily recognized by our founding fathers.

continued on pages 71 - 76

November

'Merry' Mantel Topper

Welcome Santa and all your holiday guests with a mantle bedecked in holiday colors and Christmas bells.

continued on pages 19 - 21

'Merry' Mantel Topper

designed by J. Jane Mitchell
pieced by Patsy Padgett and J. Jane Mitchell

continued from page 18

SIZE: 25" x 43"

NOTE: Measure the depth and width of your mantel to determine the size of your topper. Adjust fabric requirements and tab numbers accordingly.

Materials:

Assorted 2½" x 41" strips

5 different Green prints -

    2 strips of Green #1

    2 strips of Green #2

    2 strips of Green #3

    2 strips of Green #4

    1 strip of Green #5

5 different Red prints -

    2 strips of Red #1

    2 strips of Red #2

    2 Strips of Red #3

    2 strips of Red #4

    1 strip of Red #5

1 strip of Tan print

Batting: crib size

Fabric for the top and back of the piece that lays on the mantel 25" x 44"

Eleven 18mm bells

Crystals or other decoration for the tree

Fusible web

Rotary cutter, mat and ruler

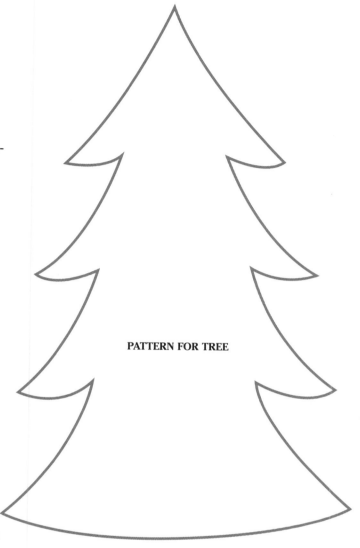

PATTERN FOR TREE

Cutting Chart:

Red #1, Green #1:

    4 - 2½" x 14" strips of <u>each</u> color. Stack 4 Greens together, 2 right side up, 2 wrong side up. Trim bottoms at a 45 degree angle. Stack and trim 4 Reds in the same manner. Cut all the rest of the strips the same way.

Red #2, Green #2:

    Four - 2½" x 13" strips, stack, cut 45 degree angle.

Red #3, Green #3:

    Four - 2½" x 12" strips, stack, cut 45 degree angle.

Red #4, Green #4:

    Four - 2½" x 11" strips, stack, cut 45 degree angle.

Red #5, Green #5:

    Four - 2½" x 10" strips, stack, cut 45 degree angle.

Tan:

    Four - 2½" x 9" strips, stack, cut 45 degree angle.

Batting:

    Eleven 5" strips the length of each of the fabric strips

        Two each - 14"; 13"; 12"; 11"; 10"

        One - 9"

    One - 12" x 43"

Yardage for piece that lays on top of the mantel:

    One - 24½" x 43½"

continued on pages 20 - 21

continued from pages 18 - 19

Construction of Topper:

With right sides together, sew a Green #1 strip to a Red #1 strip down the longest side using a ¼" seam allowance and a stitch length of 1.5.

Press seam <u>open</u>.

Trim dog ears. Repeat for all #1 strips.

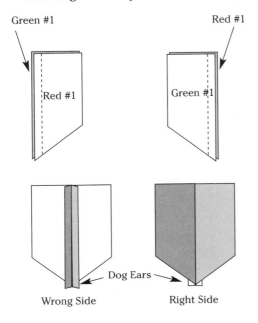

You will now have 2 sets of mirror images.

Repeat for all sets, matching Green with Red #s.

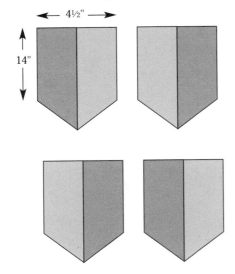

Place each set right sides together on top of a 5" x 14" piece of batting offset by ½".

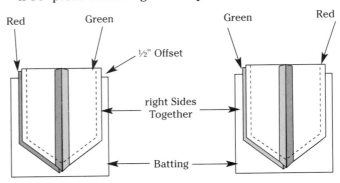

Sew around the 2 sides and bottom point using a ¼" seam allowance. Trim all 3 layers to ⅛", clip point and turn tabs right side out. Smooth outside seam and point. Press. The mirror image sets are complete.

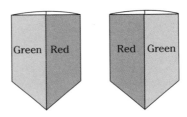

The remaining tabs will be constructed in the same manner. Two mirror images for each size tab length. You will only have one Tan tab. Set aside.

Trace the tree onto fusible web. Cut the tree out using a scant ¼" seam allowance. Iron it onto one of the Green fabric scraps following manufacturer's instructions.

Cut tree out on the traced line and fuse it to the Tan tab. Sew around the tree using a machine stitch. If you choose to hand-applique the tree, be sure to add a scant ¼" seam allowance to turn under.

Lay the fabric piece that will lay on your mantel top in front of you right side up. Place the 11 tabs, sides touching but not overlapping, wrong side up on top of the long side of fabric piece - Red side of tabs facing toward the Ecru tab. Leave a ¼" seam allowance at each end.

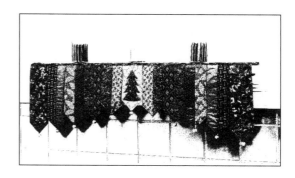

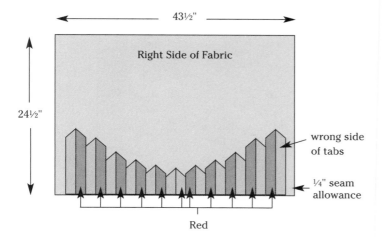

Pin tabs in place. Sew across the tabs using a scant ¼" seam allowance, being careful not to disturb the tab alignments. Fold the mantel top piece, right sides together, over the tabs.

Quilting Diagram

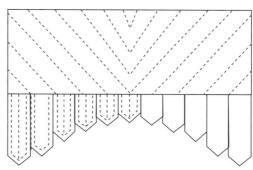

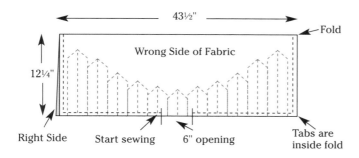

Make the bell detachable and use tassels, yo-yos or such for the second season.

It would also look nice made out of men's ties. If you used men's ties, you could make the tabs without the center seam.

Lay the tab unit on <u>top</u> of the 12" x 43½" batting piece. Start sewing on one short side using a ¼" seam allowance. Sew across the long piece leaving a 6" opening for turning. Sew the last short side. Be sure you do not catch the tabs when you are sewing the short sides.

Trim seams and batting to ⅛" except at 6" opening. Only trim the batting at the opening. Turn right side out. Smooth out seam allowance and corners. Press. Handstitch 6" opening closed. Quilt. Sew bells on tab points. Decorate the tree.

NOTE: This could easily be made reversible to be used for a different season. You would use a different backing to the mantel top and tabs.

'Ott Light' Holder
by Patsy Padgett
continued from page 4

SIZE: 4" x 4" x 15" tall

Materials:

Assorted 2½" x 41" strips:

    3 strip of Orange prints

    3 strips of Aqua prints

    1 strip of Yellow print

    1 strip of Pink print

    1 strip of Purple print

    OR we used strips from a *Moda* 'Spring Fling'
      'Jelly Roll' pack.

½ yd muslin

½ yd batting

30" cord for drawstring

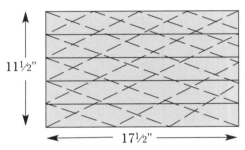

Cut quilted piece 17½" x 11½".

4. Place 11½" sides right sides together and sew a ¼" seam. Serge or zig-zag to finish raw edges. Set aside.

5. The bottom of the carrier requires a 5" square. Sew three 2½" x 5" strips together. Cut a 5" square from finished piece. This 5" square is to be quilted using same 3-layer technique as Step 3.

6. Take the carrier and sew a ¼" seam around the bottom. This will make it easier to sew the bottom 5" piece in. Fold the carrier in half using the seam line for fold on one side. Press flat all the way to the top. Matching these 2 creases, press other 2 sides flat. These 4 creases are the corners of the carrier. From the bottom of the carrier (where the ¼" seam has been sewn), cut on each fold line up to the ¼" seam line, being careful not to cut the seam line.

Using the seam line, pin one side, right sides together, to one side of the 5" square. Sew in with ¼" seam, easing as necessary. Continue around until all 4 sides are sewn. Serge or zig-zag seam to finish. Turn right side out.

7. Cut two 2" x 41" strips for carrier strap. Cut one 2" x 41" strip of batting.

Place right sides together with strip of batting on bottom. Sew strips together ¼" seam lengthwise on both sides. Turn right side out and press.

Assembly:

1. Select 6 strips. Cut each strip 2½" x 18". Sew strips together lengthwise.

2. Cut muslin 18" x 12". Cut batting 18" x 12". Cut the strip piece 18" x 12".

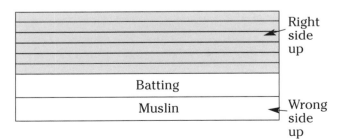

3. Layer these 3 pieces for quilting. See diagram. Quilt as desired (cross hatch, meandering, stipple, etc).

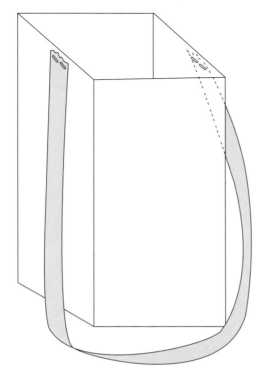

8. Place the strip right sides together to 2 sides of the holder, raw edges together. Sew in place. Set aside.

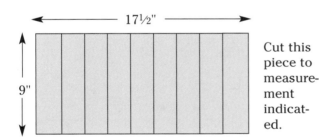

17½"

9"

Cut this piece to measurement indicated.

9. To make the top of the bag, select nine 2½" strips. Cut each strip 2½" x 9". Sew strips together lengthwise. Cut this piece to measure 9" x 17½".

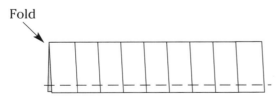

Fold

10. Fold in half right sides together and sew ¼" seam.

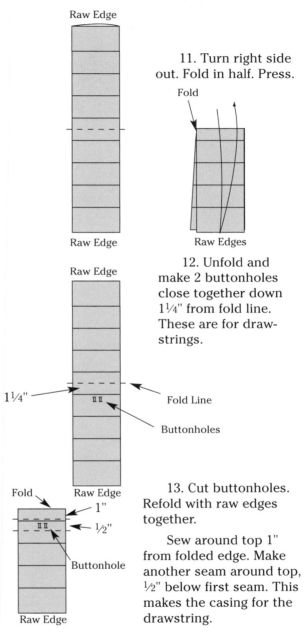

Raw Edge

Raw Edge

Raw Edges

11. Turn right side out. Fold in half. Press.

Fold

12. Unfold and make 2 buttonholes close together down 1¼" from fold line. These are for drawstrings.

Raw Edge

1¼"

Fold Line

Buttonholes

Fold   Raw Edge

1"

½"

Buttonhole

Raw Edge

13. Cut buttonholes. Refold with raw edges together.

Sew around top 1" from folded edge. Make another seam around top, ½" below first seam. This makes the casing for the drawstring.

14. Place the side with the buttonholes to the right side center front of the top of the quilted holder with raw edges together. Pin all the way around the top to ensure the top matches the holder. Sew together using ¼" seam. Serge or zig-zag to finish seam.

15. Thread the drawstring through casing. If desired, place a bead or button on the ends of the drawstring.

NOTE: I've been advised that this wonderful carrier is also useful as a knitting, magazine or wine bottle bag.

To each his own! Enjoy.

Cozy Boxes

by Patsy Padgett

continued from page 5

SIZE: 2" x 2" x 3" tall

Materials:

Assorted 2½" x 41" strips:

    3 strip of Pink print

    1 strip of Aqua print

    1 strip of Purple print

    1 strip of Yellow print

    1 strip of White print

    OR we used strips from a *Moda* 'Spring Fling' 'Jelly Roll' 2½" x 41" strips pack.

Thread

Batting

Assembly:

1. Select two complementary fabric strips.

2. Fold each fabric piece wrong sides together.

3. Make a template of the pattern.

4. Lay template on fabric and cut 2 strips of each fabric. You will now have 4 single pieces of each fabric.

5. Lay template on batting and cut 4 pieces.

6. Take 1 piece of each fabric and place right sides together. Lay pieces on 1 piece of batting.

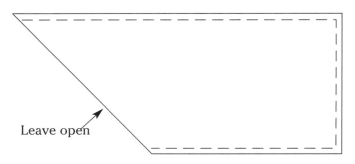

Leave open

7. Sew 3 layers together around 3 sides, leaving diagonal cut end open.

8. Sew the other 3 sets as in Step 7.

9. After sewing all 4 sets, turn 1 right side out, being very careful not to stretch the diagonal cut end.

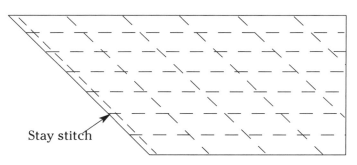

Stay stitch

10. Press.

11. Quilt all 4 strips. This is a good time to stay stitch the diagonal cut end to prevent stretching.

See diagram above.

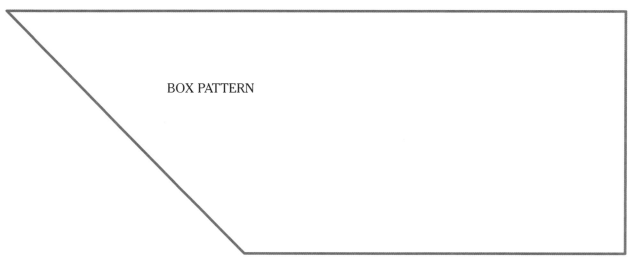

BOX PATTERN

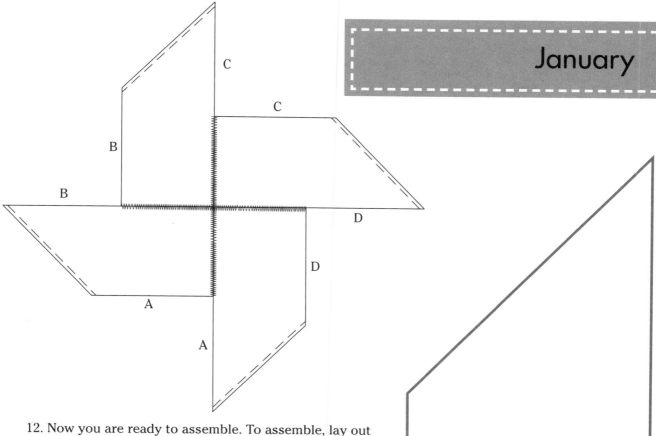

12. Now you are ready to assemble. To assemble, lay out the 4 quilted pieces as per diagram.

13. Zig-zag strips together. This forms the bottom of the cozy box.

14. Place long sides AA, BB, CC, DD together, one at a time. Slipstitch as you place each 2 sides together.

See diagram below.

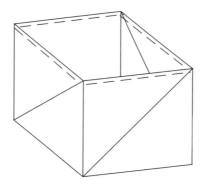

15. Cut a 2¼" strip long enough to go around the top of the cozy box. Fold in half lengthwise with right sides together. Press.

16. Place raw edges of the binding to raw edge of the cozy box and sew together with a ¼" seam. Fold the folded edge of the binding to the inside of the cozy box and slipstitch in place.

Your cozy box may be embellished with lace, fringe, beads, etc. The little 2½" x 2½" Omnigrid will fit in the bottom of your box.

NOTE: When making the can cozy, use insulated batting. You might want to cut a 2½" x 2½" square of cork or coaster material to put in the bottom of your cozy.

COZY PATTERN

'Hugs and Kisses' Table Topper

designed by J. Jane Mitchell
pieced by Patsy Padgett

continued from page 6

SIZE: 16" x 32"

FINISHED BLOCK: 5¾" x 5¾"

Materials:

6 strips 2½" x 41" (Red to Pink)

1 strip 2½" x 41" Red tone on tone

3 strips 2½" x 41" White with Red print

 OR we used strips from *Moda* 'Hearts A Flutter' 'Jelly Roll' 2½" x 41" strips collection.

Backing 18" x 34"

Batting 18" x 34"

Wrights Easy Angle cutting ruler

Rotary cutter and mat

Copies of paper piecing

Cutting Chart

Refer to photo of sample for color placement ideas.

Reds to Pinks - Cut (24) 2½" x 2½" squares

Reds to Pinks - Cut (72) 2½" half square triangles

Red tone on tone - Cut 2½" x 41" strip in half lengthwise, then subcut
 4 - 1¼" x 4½" (O's #10, 12);
 4 - 1¼" x 3½" (O's #11, 13);
 8 - 1¼" x 1" (O's #6, 7, 8, 9);
 2 - 1¼" x 4¾" (X's #8);
 4 - 1¼" x 2¼" (X's #4, 12)

White with Red print - Cut
 10 - 1½" x 1½" squares (O's #1; X's #1, 5, 10, 14)

Cut strips in half lengthwise, then subcut
 8 - 1¼" x 6" (O's #20, 21; X's #18, 19);
 8 - 1¼" x 4¾" (O's #18, 20; X's #16, 17);
 4 - 1¼" x 3¼" (O's #4, 5);
 20 - 1¼" x 1½" (O's #2, 3, 14, 15, 16, 17; X's #2, 6, 9, 13);
 8 - 1¼" x 2½" (X's #3, 7, 11, 15)

Piecing:

Lay out pieces for each heart in front of you in the order that they will be sewn.

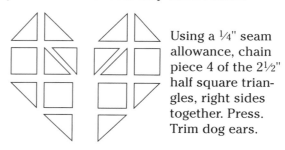

Using a ¼" seam allowance, chain piece 4 of the 2½" half square triangles, right sides together. Press. Trim dog ears.

Next place them back in their correct places.

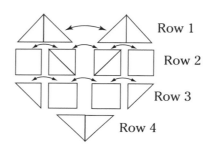

Row 1
Row 2
Row 3
Row 4

Sew Row 1 together.
Press seams open.

Sew Row 2 together.
Press seams to the right.

Sew Row 3 together. Trim dog ears.
Press seams to the left.

Sew Row 1 to Row 2.
Press seams down.

Sew Row 3 to row 4.
Press seams down.

Sew Row 2 to Row 3.
Press seams down.

 Complete 5 remaining hearts in the same manner. Set aside.

Paper Pieced Blocks:

 Refer to Log Cabin Place Mats on page 71 for basic paper piecing instructions.

Additional Instructions for the X's:

The X's use 4 steps to complete

Step 1 - Presew together, then place on paper piecer
   #1 - 1½" x 1½" square to #2 - 1¼" x 1½" piece
   #5 - 1½" x 1½" square to #6 - 1¼" x 1½" piece
   #9 - 1½" x 1½" square to #10 - 1¼" x 1½" piece
   #13 - 1½" x 1½" square to #14 - 1¼" x 1½" piece

Step 2 - Paper piece Part 1 and Part 2.

Step 3 - Join Part 1and Part 2 at arrows, making sure the Reds match so your X's will form correctly.

Step 4 - Sew the 4 White with Red print strips around outside edges (#16, 17, 18, 19).

Note: These are not paper pieced, but are added to your paper pieced Part 1 and Part 2 that have already been joined.

You may remove all of your paper or you may want to remove just the outside 4 strips until the topper is all sewn together. It's up to you.

Joining the Blocks:

Join on the diagonal.

Join Row 1. Press.

Join Row 2. Press.

Join Row 3. Press.

Join Row 4. Press.

Now you will have some strange look-ing seams. Do not be afraid of these.

Treat the seam between Row 1 and Row 2 as two separate seams.

Sew the short seam between the top 2 hearts, stopping and backtacking right at the top tip of the White on the X block.

Remove this piece from the sewing machine.

Sew a seam from the top of the X tip down to the heart (Diagram A).

Press.

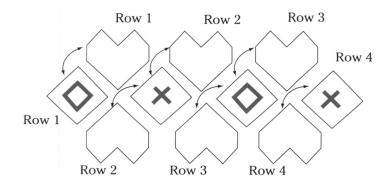

Diagram A

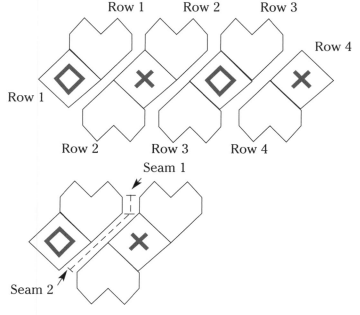

continued on pages 28 - 31

continued from pages 24 - 27

Diagram B

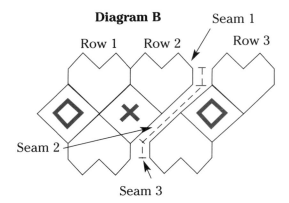

Sew Row 2 to Row 3. This time you will treat it as 3 seams (Diagram B).

Sew Seam 1.

Remove from machine. Sew Seam 2.

Remove from machine. Sew Seam 3.

Press.

Diagram C

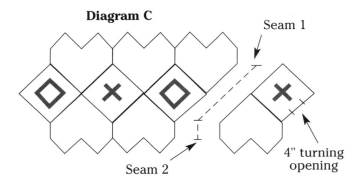

Now you are ready to join Row 3 and Row 4. Treat it as you did Row 1 and Row 2, using 2 seams (Diagram C).

Press.

continued on pages 28 - 29

Sample Quilting Pattern

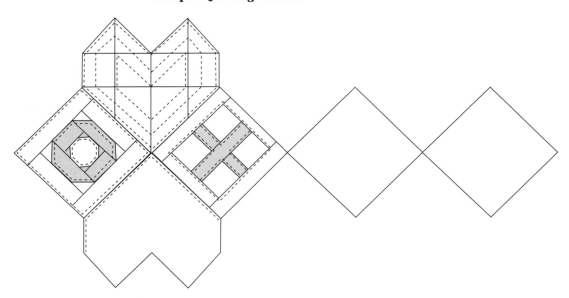

Layering the Topper:

Place the batting down first. Place the lining right side up facing you on top of the batting. Place the heart top right side down onto backing. Pin in place. Sew using ¼" seam allowance around the entire top except for a 4" turning opening on the last X block (see Diagram C).

Trim batting, backing and top to a scant ¼" seam allowance, except at 4" turning opening. At the opening only trim the batting. This will allow enough fabric to sew the opening closed.

Trim points and clip where necessary.

Remember in 'piecing section' where you were told to press the seam open on Row 1 between the top of the heart sections. If you did this it gave you a guide so you could sew exactly to the 'dip' in the heart and when turned this seam will automatically come open so your piece will be flat.

Turn your piece right side out. Ease out all tips and seams. Press. Handstitch 4" opening closed. Quilt your topper.

NOTE: Depending on the size of your table, you may keep adding hearts and O's and X's to fit. Adjust yardage accordingly.

Hugs and Kisses to you!

Red Tone on Tone
color fabric

Make 2 copies of the pattern below
Sewing Line _____
Seam Allowance - - - - - - - - - - - - - - -
The center square (1) uses one 1½" x 1½" square

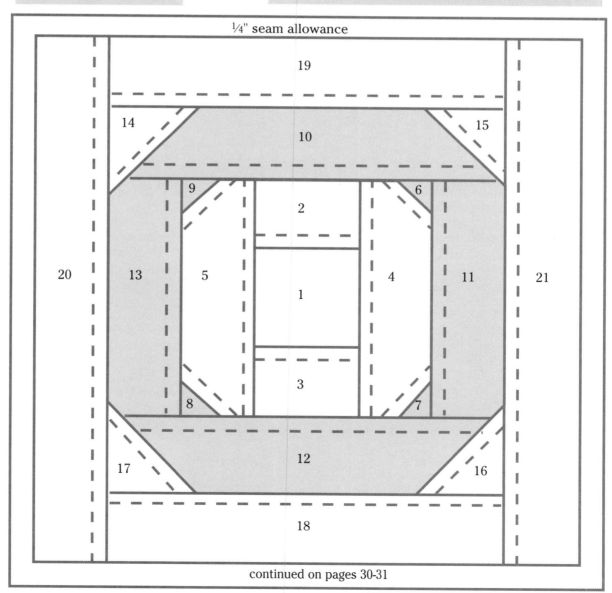

continued on pages 30-31

continued from pages 24 - 29

Red Tone on Tone
color fabric

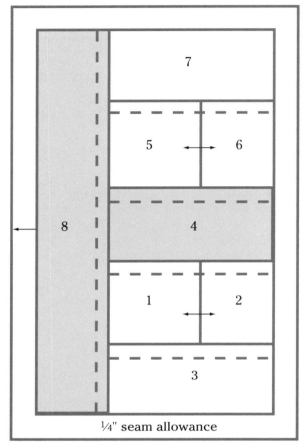

¼" seam allowance

Paper Piecing - cut 2

Make 2 copies of each pattern
Sewing Line _____
Seam Allowance - - - - - - - -

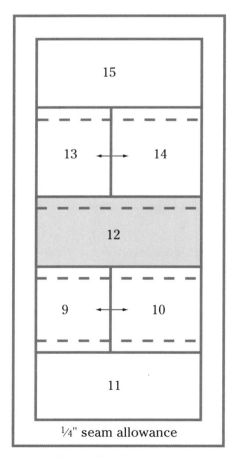

¼" seam allowance

Paper Piecing - cut 2

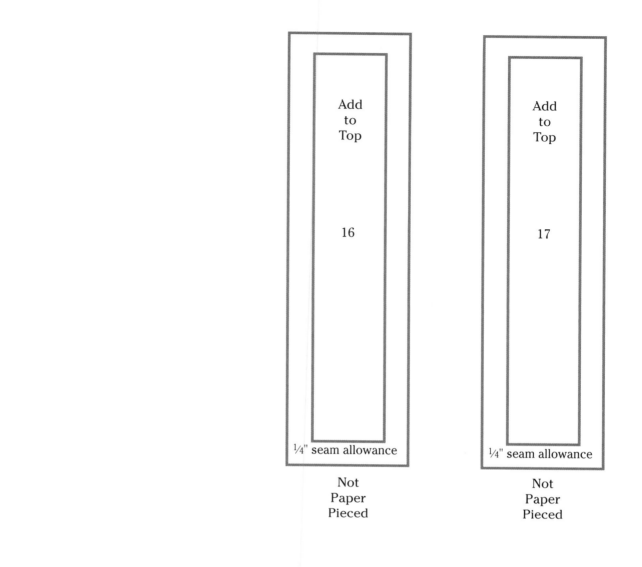

Add
to
Top

16

¼" seam allowance

Not
Paper
Pieced

Add
to
Top

17

¼" seam allowance

Not
Paper
Pieced

18

Add
to
Side

¼" seam allowance

Not Paper Pieced

19

Add
to
Side

¼" seam allowance

Not Paper Pieced

'Birds in the Air'
Wall Hanging or Table Topper

by J. Jane Mitchell

continued from page 7

WALL HANGING: 27" x 27"

FINISHED BLOCK: 6" x 6"

Materials:

3 coordinating 2½" x 41" strips of Red

3 coordinating 2½" x 41" strips of Blue

3 coordinating 2½" x 41" strips of Green

One 2½" x 41" strip of Ivory

6 coordinating 2½" x 41" strips of Ecru
   to go with Blue, Green, Peach and Brown strips

2 coordinating 2½" x 41" strips of Peach

2 coordinating 2½" x 41" strips of Brown

Four 2½" x 41" strips for binding (2 Reds and 2 Blues)
   OR we used strips from a *Moda* 'Folklorique'
      'Jelly Roll' 2½" x 41" strips pack

29" x 29" batting

29" x 29" backing

Hanging sleeve 9" x 28"

Wrights Easy Angle ruler

Rotary cutter with mat

Templastic (for making your own template)

Black permanent marker

Cutting Chart:

The Easy Angle ruler is used to cut half square triangles out of a 2½" wide strip. Follow instructions on package. Make template #1 and #2 from templastic. Remove selvages.

Red color 1: Cut sixteen 2½" half square triangles using Easy Angle ruler.

Red color 2: Cut 4 using template #1.

Red color 3: Cut 4 using template #2.

Blue color 1: Cut 16 - 2½" half square triangles using Easy Angle ruler.

Blue color 2: Cut 4 using template #1.

Blue color 3: Cut 4 using template #2.

Green color 1: Cut 16 - 2½" half square triangles using Easy Angle ruler.

Green color 2: Cut 4 using template #1.

Green color 3: Cut 4 using template #2.

Ivory: Cut 24 - 2½" half square triangles using Easy Angle ruler.

Ecru: Cut 120 - 2½" half square triangles using Easy Angle ruler.

Brown color 1: Cut 9 - 2½" half square triangles using Easy Angle ruler.

Brown color 2: Cut 9 - 2½" half square triangles using Easy Angle ruler.

Peach color 1: Cut 9 - 2½" half square triangles using Easy Angle ruler.

Peach color 2: Cut 9 - 2½" half square triangles using Easy Angle ruler.

Assembly of the Blocks:

Unit 1: Sew 3 Light half square triangles and 3 Red half square triangles, right sides together, using a ¼" seam allowance. Press toward the Red. Trim dog ears.

Sew

Press

Dog Ears

Sew two finished squares together. Sew a Ivory half square triangle to the two finished squares. Press. Trim dog ears.

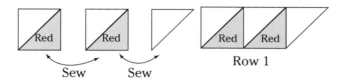

Take the remaining finished square and sew an Ivory half square triangle to it. Press. Trim dog ears.

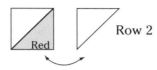

Join Row 1 and Row 2, right sides together.

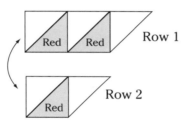

Add the last Light half square triangle to bottom of Row 2, right sides together. Press. Make 4 total.

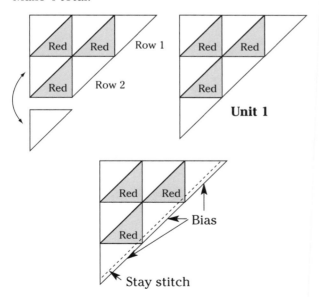

Do these same steps with the Green and Ecru, Blue and Ecru, Brown and Ecru, and Peach and Ecru half square triangles. Handle carefully. These unit 1's all have bias bottoms. You would be wise to staystitch them a scant ¼".

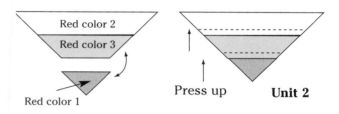

Unit 2: Sew 4 Red color 2 and color 3 strips, right sides together.

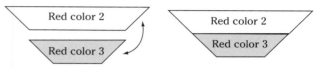

Add the last 4 Red color 1 half square triangles to the bottom of Red color 3's, right sides together. Press up toward Red #2. Trim dog ears.

Do these same steps with the Green colors #2, 3, 1 and the Blue colors #2, 3, 1.

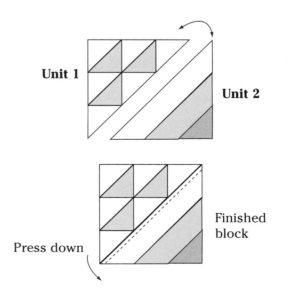

Join units 1 and 2 of the Reds, Blues and Greens, right sides together. Press down toward Unit 2.

continued on pages 34 - 36

continued from pages 32 - 33

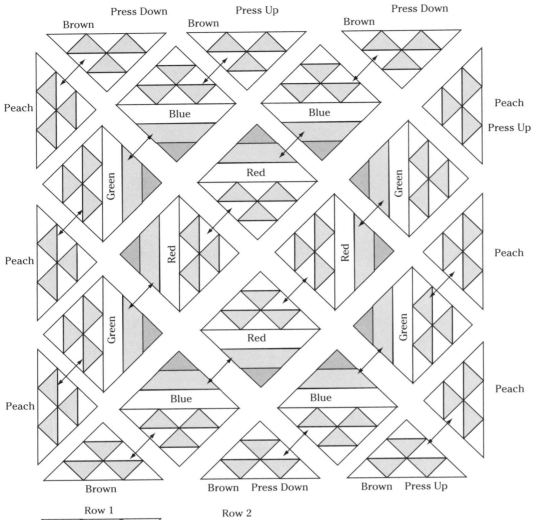

Joining Rows:

The blocks will be set on point, so you will need to join the rows diagonally. Lay out finished blocks and extra Units 1 in this order.

See Diagram. Join blocks and units 1 in arrow order, right sides together. Press each row in opposite directions. Handle gently.

See Diagram. Join Rows 1, 2, & 3 right sides together. Press.

Join Rows 4, 5, & 6 right sides together. Press.

Join Rows 3 & 4 right sides together. Press.

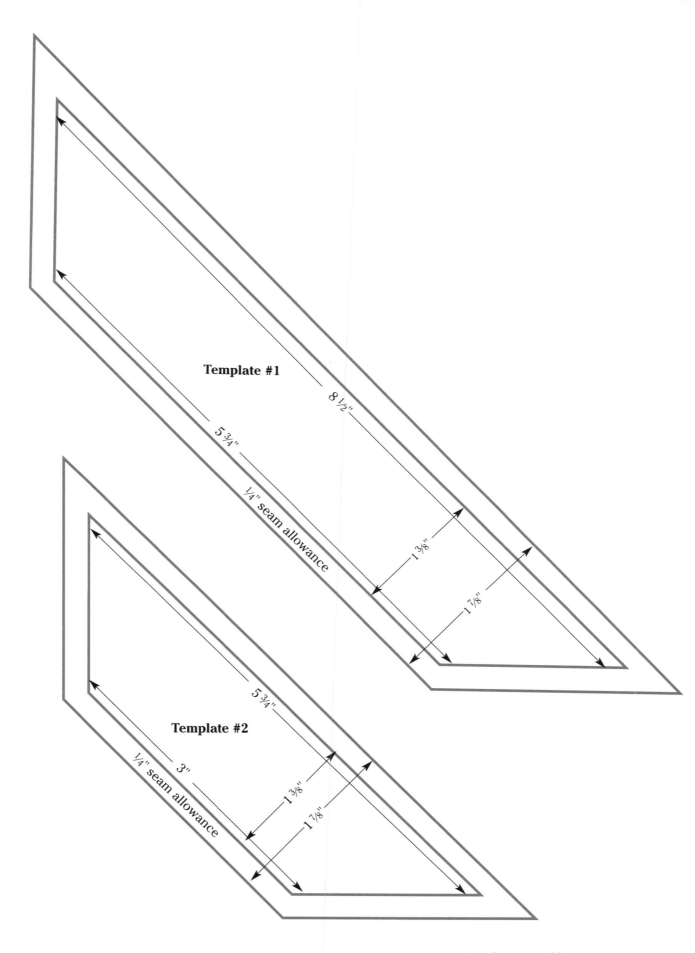

Template #1

8 ½"

5 ¾"

¼" seam allowance

1 ⅜"

1 ⅞"

Template #2

5 ¾"

3"

¼" seam allowance

1 ⅜"

1 ⅞"

continued on page 36

continued from pages 32 - 35

Quilting:

See Diagram for how the wall hanging was quilted in the ditch.

Pat yourself on the back. You have now finished your top.

Now you need to layer it for quilting. Lay the backing out right side down. Place the batting on top of the backing. Lay the top onto batting right side up.

Secure the 3 layers so they will not shift. You could masking tape your backing to a protected table top or the floor.

Safety pin baste the backing, batting and top if you plan to machine quilt it or thread baste them if you plan to handquilt it. Quilt it.

Binding:

Refer to the Log Cabin Place Mat on page 71 for the binding instructions.

Hanging Sleeve Instructions:

Cut a piece of fabric 28" long by 9" wide. Turn under ¼" on each end. Press, then turn under ¼" again and sew on the machine.

Sew together wrong sides facing using a ½" seam allowance along the longest side to form a tube.

Press ½" seam allowance open rolling it to the back center of the tube.

Handsew this tube (top, bottom and ends) to the back top of the quilt just under the binding, with the seam allowance toward the back of the quilt.

Do not handstitch the tube closed at the ends. Just stitch the ends of the tube that are next to the back of the quilt. Do not let your stitches go through to the front of the quilt. Just sew through backing and batting.

Your quilt is now ready to hang.

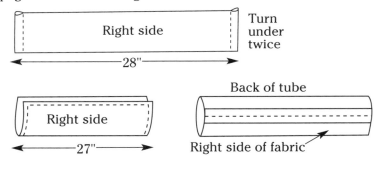

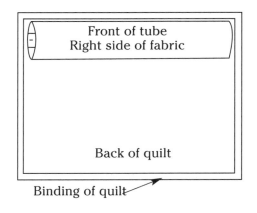

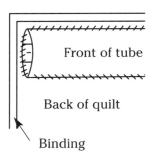

'Happy' Apron

by Patsy Padgett

continued from page 8

SIZE: 24" x 33"

Materials:

2 strips 2½" x 41" of Orange prints

3 strips 2½" x 41" of Green prints

1 strip 2½" x 41" of Yellow print

3 strips 2½" x 41" of Pink prints

    OR we used strips from a *Moda* 'Spring Fling'

      'Jelly Roll' 2½" x 41" strips pack

      (one pack is enough for more than one apron)

1 yd muslin

½ yd fabrics for pockets and binding

Assembly:

1. Lay pattern on fold of muslin and cut one apron.

2. Open apron leaving center fold line intact. The center line is very important in the construction of the apron. The apron is constructed on the wrong side of the muslin.

3. Cut one 4" strip from one 'jelly roll' strip. Center 4" strip on the top of the bib of apron, right side up. Sew a scant ¼" seam across the top of the bib. This will hold your 4" strip in place.

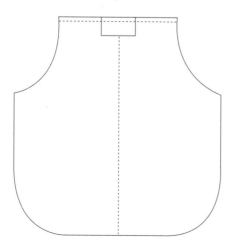

4. Draw a 45 degree angle line from 'A' to top of bib. This is a very important step.

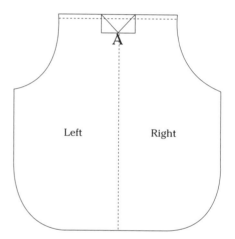

5. Cut one 2½" x 5" strip. Place edge of strip along left line, right sides together. Sew a ¼" seam from top of bib to center line of apron.

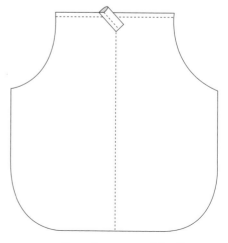

continued on pages 38 - 41

continued from page 37

6. Flip and press, being careful to leave the center crease intact.

7. Cut one 2½" x 7" strip. Place strip on right side of apron along second 45 degree angle line, right sides together. Sew a ¼" seam from top of bib to edge of first strip. Flip and press.

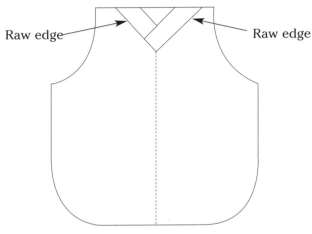

Raw edge ⟶   ⟵ Raw edge

8. Cut one 2½" x 7" strip. Place on raw edge of first strip, right sides together. Sew a ¼" seam to the center of apron. Flip and press.

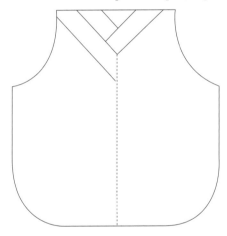

9. Cut a 2½" x 9" strip. Place on raw edge of second strip, right sides together. Sew a ¼" seam to edge of last strip sewn. Flip and press.

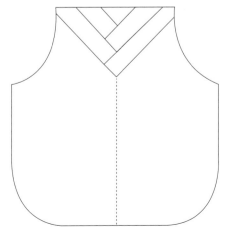

10. Cutting longer strips each time, continue Steps 8 and 9 until apron is completely covered.

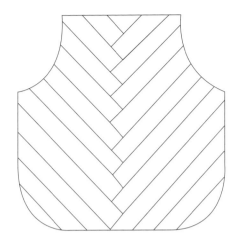

11. Turn apron to wrong side and trim excess strips off.

Bias Edging:

12. Cut 2½" bias strips from the ½ yard piece. You will need approximately 5½ yards of bias strip. After sewing all strips together, fold right sides together and press.

13. Cut a strip of bias long enough to cover top edge of apron bib. Place raw edges of bias strip to raw edges of wrong side of apron bib. Sew a ¼" seam across top of bib.

Fold folded edge of bias strip to front side of apron. Covering previous seam, sew close to folded edge to finish top of bib.

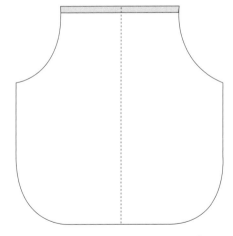

14. Cut a strip of bias long enough to go around lower part of apron. Place raw edges of bias strip to raw edge of wrong side of lower part of apron. Sew a ¼" seam.

Fold folded edge of bias strip to front side of apron. Covering previous seam, sew close to folded edge of bias strip to finish lower part of the apron.

15. The remainder of the bias strip will be used to bind the remainder of the apron's unfinished edges, and to make the ties as well as the tie around the neck.

16. Measure 35" from one end of bias strip. At this point place raw edges of bias strip to the raw edge of the wrong side of the apron. Sew a ¼" seam to top of bib of apron.

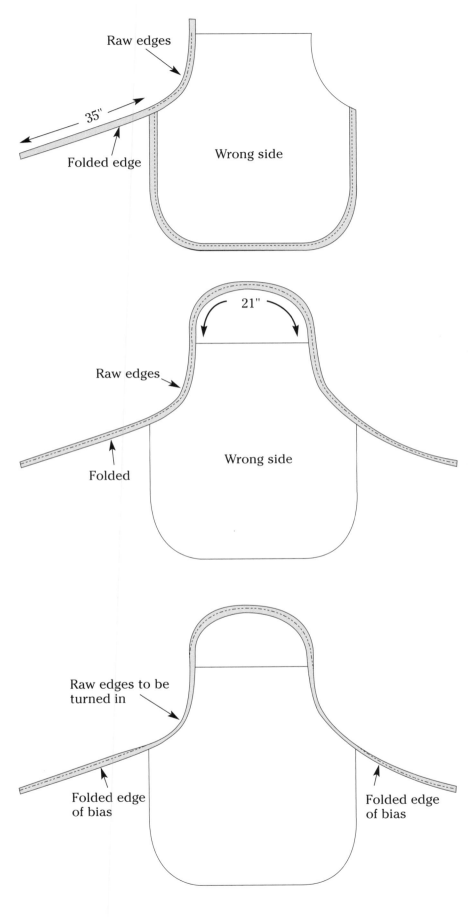

17. Measure 21" from this point and sew the second side.

18. Fold folded edge of bias strip to front side of apron. Covering previous seam, sew close to folded edge on both sides of the apron.

19. Use the ¼" seam line stitching as your fold line. Fold in and press. Bring the two folded edges together and stitch close to folded edges to finish the ties and neck edges. Measure the ties and ensure they are the same length. If not, cut to same length.

Pocket:

20. Cut a pocket from remaining fabric used to cut bias strips. You should have enough to cut two pockets if desired. Turn top of pocket down 1¼" to wrong side. Turn under ¼" around rest of pocket and press.

Try on the apron and place a pocket in the desired position. Pin in place. Sew pocket on apron.

continued on pages 40 - 41

continued from pages 37 - 39

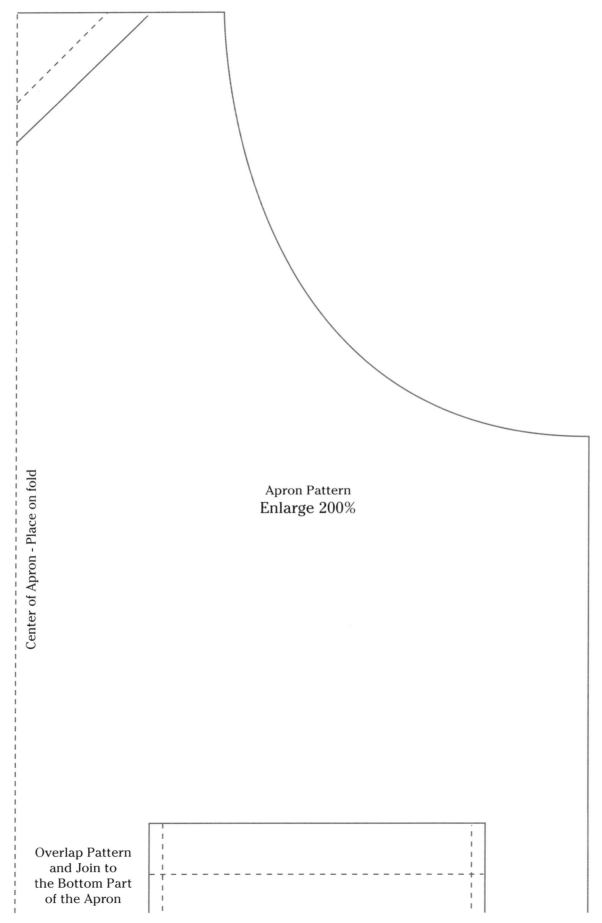

Center of Apron - Place on fold

Apron Pattern
Enlarge 200%

Overlap Pattern
and Join to
the Bottom Part
of the Apron

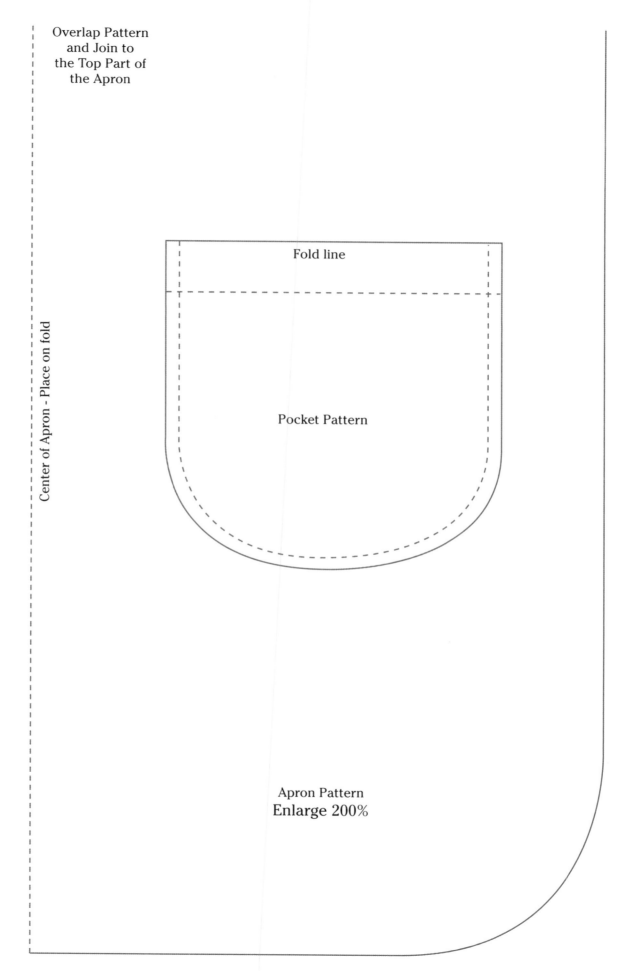

Overlap Pattern
and Join to
the Top Part of
the Apron

Center of Apron - Place on fold

Fold line

Pocket Pattern

Apron Pattern
Enlarge 200%

'Batik Beauties' Wall Hanging
by J. Jane Mitchell

continued from page 9

SIZE: 27½" x 27½"

Materials:

Assorted batik fabric strips 2½" x 41":

- 4 strips of assorted Browns (basket)
- 1½ Light Green strips (table top)
- 8 Cream strips for background
- 4 dark strips, 2 light strips (borders and corner sets)
- 4 different Green strips, or variegated Green strips (leaves)
- 5 strips assorted Blues & Purples(flowers)
- Scraps of Yellow (flower centers)
- 3 strips for binding

30" x 30" batting (plus scraps for leaves)

30" x 30" backing

Rotary cutter

6" x 24" ruler

23" x 35" gridded mat

Pinking shears or pinking rotary blade

Hot glue gun

"Stiffy" fabric stiffener

Template material

Permanent marker

Chalk wheel

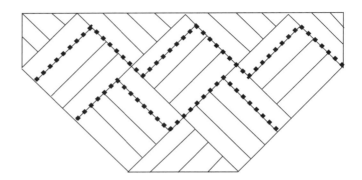

Basket - Cutting Chart:

Cut the 4 Brown strips in half lengthwise.

Subcut 10 - 1¼" x 3½" strips from each color.

Number the 4 Brown stacks from 1 o 4, Dark to Light.

Background, Borders & Corners - Cutting Chart:

Refer to Diagram A. Diagram A Cutting Chart includes ¼" seam allowances, background, borders and corner squares.

Leaves - Cutting Chart:

8-10 large #3 for top of leaf

8-10 large #3 for bottom of leaf

8-10 medium #2

6-8 small #1

Batting for large #3 leaves

Flowers - Cutting Chart:

Refer to flower construction under each type of flower on pages 45 - 46.

Diagram A

NOTE: Cut your longest background strips first.
. . . . **quilting lines**

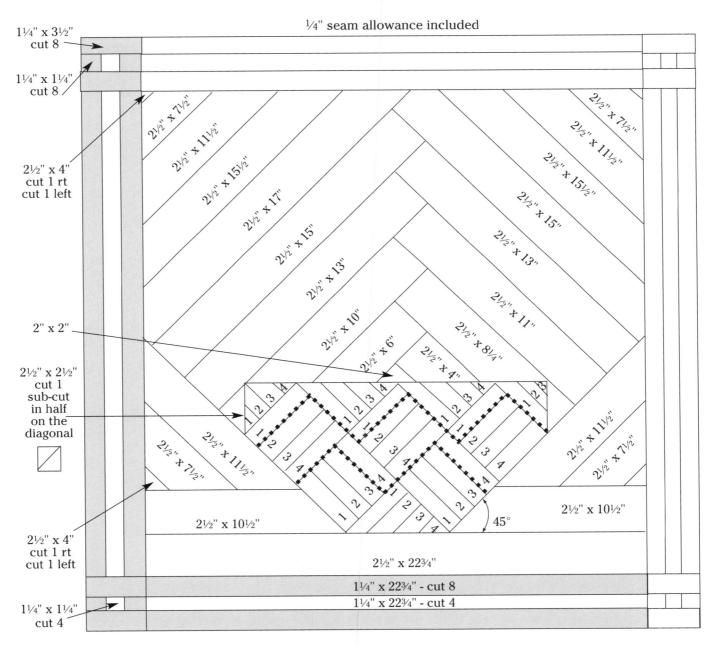

¼" seam allowance included

1¼" x 3½"
cut 8

1¼" x 1¼"
cut 8

2½" x 4"
cut 1 rt
cut 1 left

2" x 2"

2½" x 2½"
cut 1
sub-cut
in half
on the
diagonal

2½" x 7½"

2½" x 11½"

2½" x 15½"

2½" x 17"

2½" x 15"

2½" x 13"

2½" x 10"

2½" x 6"

2½" x 4"

2½" x 8¼"

2½" x 11"

2½" x 13"

2½" x 15"

2½" x 15½"

2½" x 11½"

2½" x 7½"

2½" x 11½"

2½" x 7½"

2½" x 7½"

2½" x 11½"

45°

2½" x 10½"

2½" x 10½"

2½" x 22¾"

1¼" x 22¾" - cut 8

1¼" x 22¾" - cut 4

2½" x 4"
cut 1 rt
cut 1 left

1¼" x 1¼"
cut 4

28" x 28" seam allowance included (27½" x 27½" finished)
background, borders and corner squares

continued on pages 44 - 47

continued from pages 42 - 43

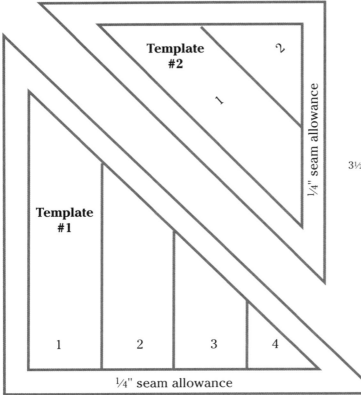

Template
#2

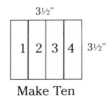

¼" seam allowance

Template
#1

1   2   3   4

¼" seam allowance

BATIK BEAUTIES

BASKET
TEMPLATES

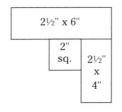

Template
#3

1   2   3   4

¼" seam allowance

Construction of Basket:

Make 10 - 3½" x 3½" squares from the 4 Brown fabrics numbering from 1 to 4. Use a ¼" seam allowance.

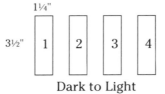

Dark to Light

Make Ten

Set aside 5 complete squares. Trace basket templates #1, 2, 3 onto template material using permanent marker. Be sure to trace numbers and lines also.

Lay template #1 on top of one of the extra 5 squares, matching numbers and sewing lines. Trace around it and cut it out on traced line. Do this 2 more times.

Lay template #2 on one of the two remaining squares, matching sewing lines and numbers. Trace around it and cut out on traced line.

Lay template #3 on last square, matching sewing lines and numbers. Trace around it. Cut out on traced line.

Construct the basket by sewing blocks and triangles together using ¼" seam allowances.

Refer to Diagram A on page 40 for proper placements.

Set aside.

Construction of Background:

Starting with the pieces just above the basket, sew the 2" x 2" square to the side of the 2½" x 4" strip.

Sew the 2½" x 6" strip to the top.

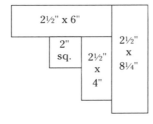

Sew the 2½" x 8¼" strip to the side.

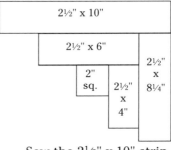

Sew the 2½" x 10" strip to the top.

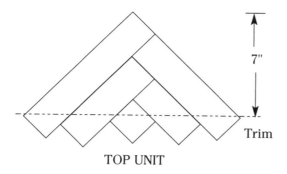

TOP UNIT

Take this unit, with the long side at the bottom using the 45 degree angle on the ruler, trim it to 7" at the peak.

Add the two background triangles to each side of the basket unit. Center them. Press. Trim dog ears.

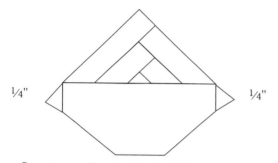

Sew top unit onto basket. Press seams down. Square this unit up to be 11". Be careful not to trim the ¼" seam allowance off.

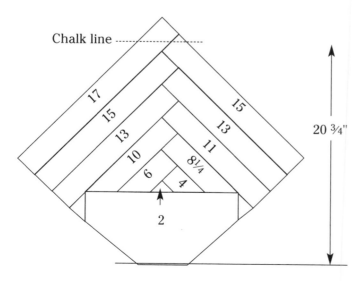

Continue adding strips alternately to the top of the unit (first to the right side and then to the left) until you have added the 2½" x 17" strip.

At this point, measure the piece from the bottom of the basket to the top of the unit. Do this by laying the unit on the gridded mat with bottom on one of the grid lines.

With the ruler, measure up from the bottom 20¾". Using the chalk wheel, make a line across the top.

Cut top off on the chalk line.

Continue adding strips alternately to top unit, offsetting them ¼" seam allowance above chalk line.

You will have to make a new chalk line as you add more strips. Continue in this manner until you have added all of the strips, ending with the 2½" x 4" strips. The sides will be jagged like the top. Press seams up. Set aside.

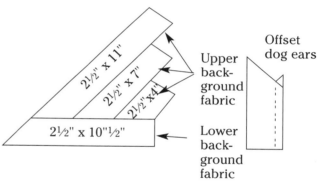

Construct the units that go on either side of the basket. Sew the 2½" x 11½" strip to the 2½" x 7½" strip, offsetting the point by ¼". Sew the 2½" x 4" strip to the 2½" x 7", offsetting the points by ¼". Right sides together, sew the 2½" x 10½" lower background strip to the bottom of last unit.

Press to the right and down. Trim dog ears.

Sew the opposite unit. Sew these two units to either side of basket unit. Keep Diagram A close at hand for easy reference.

Sew the last lower background strip to the bottom of the large unit, centering it to center of basket bottom.

Press seam downward.

Square the whole background unit up to 22¾" x 22¾". Set aside.

continued on pages 46 - 47

continued from pages 42 - 45

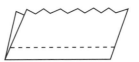

Construction of Borders and Corner Blocks:

Sew a Dark 1¼" x 22¾" strip on either side of a Light 1¼" x 22¾" strip. Gently press toward the dark strips. Do this 3 more times.

Sew a border strip to either side of the background unit. For the corner blocks, sew a Dark 1¼" square to either side of a Light 1¼" square. Press toward the Dark.

Do this 3 more times. Next sew a Dark 1¼" x 3½" strip to the top and bottom of these 4 units. Press towards the Dark.

Sew a corner unit to each end of the last two border strips. Sew the completed 2 border strips to the top and bottom of the background unit.

Layering, Quilting and Binding:

Lay the 30" x 30" backing right side down. Lay the batting on top of the backing. Lay the wall hanging top onto batting right side up. Pin in place. Quilt.

The sample was machine quilted 'in the ditch' of all background seams, around basket and all border seams. The basket was quilted 'in the ditch' along marked seams. Refer to dots on Diagram A.

Cut the three 2½" wide binding strips down to 2¼" wide. Sew together on the diagonal end to end. Press in half lengthwise. Refer to the 'Log Cabin' Place Mats on page 71 for the binding instructions.

Don't forget to put a hanging sleeve on it. The instructions for that are in the 'Birds in the Air' wall hanging on page 36.

Flower Construction:
Largest Flowers

With pinking shears or rotary pinking blade, cut on both long sides of a 2½" x 41" strip. (Some of the flowers were torn on the edges instead of pinked.)

Fold the fabric in half lengthwise. Sew by hand a basting stitch about ¼" up from folded edge.

Use a strong cotton/poly-wrapped thread, so it will not break when you gather it up, knotted at one end.

When you start gathering the strip, begin to wrap it around itself. Gather it very tight. When it is all gathered and wrapped around itself, hold it in your fist right side down and whipstitch the rows or gathered rounds together. This takes quite a bit of stitching.

You will know you are finished when you turn it right side up and cannot see daylight through the rows.

Next separate the folded strip to make it fuller.

Medium and Small Flowers:

These can be made like the largest flowers, but cutting your strip shorter and narrower. Another technique is to sew the basting stitch down the center of the strip without folding it.

After you gather this up very tight and tie it off, twist the front and back in opposite directions. This will flatten the flower.

Then you can make a smaller one and place it on the larger one for a very cute center. On some of the smaller flowers I used a Gold thread that I had left a long tail on the knot to gather the strips with. This gives the illusion of a stamen in the center.

By using different lengths and widths of strips, you can create many unusual flowers. You really just need to play with them and have fun. The length of the basting stitches changes the look also. I used around a ¼" long stitch.

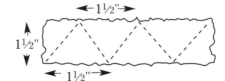

Ruching Flower:s

With a 1½" strip, sew basting stitches in a zig-zag pattern down the length of the strip. The ones I made used about a 4" long strip. Pull the basting thread to gather it up. Tack it closed.

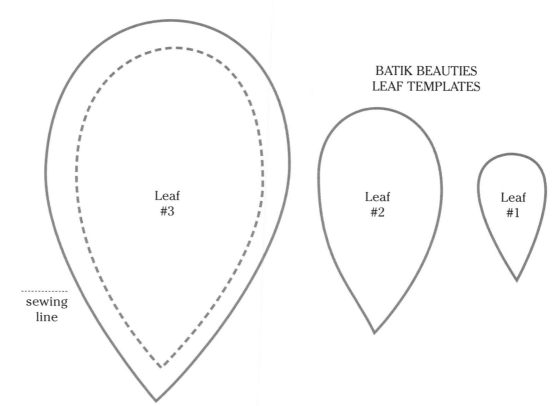

BATIK BEAUTIES
LEAF TEMPLATES

Leaf
#3

Leaf
#2

Leaf
#1

sewing
line

Flower Buds:

Use a 1" wide strip and fold the corner down before you roll or gather it. Do this looser than when forming a large flower.

Or just roll a strip and then snip it to make it fluffy and stick it down in the center of another flower after sewing or wrapping thread around the rolled end.

Large Leaves #3:

The large #3 leaves were made with a top fabric and a bottom fabric, with batting in between.

Make a template. Trace 2 patterns for each leaf.

Cut a piece of batting at least ¼" smaller all the way around. Place the batting inside the 2 leaf patterns. Sew on the top of your leaf about a ¼" seam allowance in from the outside edge. These are raw edges.

Then sew a vein down the middle and smaller ones too if you prefer. Trim the back of the leaf close to the stitching line. Using pinking tool, pink just the front edge all the way around, not too close to the stitching.

Medium Leaves #2 and Small Leaves #1:

Make a template for each #2 and #1 leaf.

Trace them onto a single thickness of fabric if you are doing selective cutting. Cut them out with pinking tool.

Using the fabric stiffener, follow the manufacturer's instructions to apply it to the leaves. While they are still damp, curve and shape them.

After they are dry, you will be ready to make your flower arrangement.

Arranging Flowers and Leaves:

This wall hanging will never be washed so I used hot glue to attach the flowers and leaves to the background. I think it would be rather difficult to sew them on without distorting the background, but you are welcome to try if you have an aversion to hot glue.

Refer to the photo of the sample for flower placement. Have fun with your arrangement - it doesn't have to look like the sample!

My sweet mother-in-law was very kind to share her talent of flower arranging with me. I hope you enjoy making this wall hanging and will use it to brighten your home, or that of someone you love.

Have fun with your arrangement!

Watermelon Place Mat

by Donna Kinsey

continued from page 11

SIZE: 12" x 18"

Materials:

6 Red print 2½" x 18" strips

Green fabric for bias edging 18" x 18"

White fabric for bias edging 18" x 18"

Backing fabric 12" x 18"

DMC #310 Black pearl cotton

Cutting:

Red: Cut 6 strips 2½" x 18"

Pattern: Copy and enlarge pattern 200%.

Backing: Cut out watermelon pattern.

Bias Edging: Cut across the diagonal of each fabric

    Cut Green strips: 2¼" wide

    Cut White strips: ¾" wide

Assemble Bias Strips:

Sew the ends together to make 42" of bias strip.

Sew the Green strip to the White strip.

Assembly:

With right sides together, sew the first strip to the top edge of the place mat. Trim seam to ⅛".

Turn strip 1 to the back of the mat and press. Topstitch along the edge of the place mat.

Strip 2: With right sides together, place strip 2 over strip 1 aligning the raw edge. Sew a ¼" seam. Fold back strip 2. Press.

Continue adding strips 3, 4, 5 and 6 until all 6 strips are sewn in place.

Finishing:

Turn the place mat over to the back and sew a line ⅛" from the edge around the curve to stabilize the edge.

With right sides together, position the White strip against the curved edge of the place mat, folding down a ½" hem at the top edge.

TIP: Ease the white edge of the bias strip as you pin and sew it to the place mat. This bit of easement will allow the bias edging to lay flat after you turn it to the back.

Sew binding in place with a ¼" seam.

Fold bias edging in half lengthwise along the edge. Press.

Fold binding to the back and Blindstitch in place.

Using Black pearl cotton, embroider Lazy Daisy stitches to represent watermelon seeds.

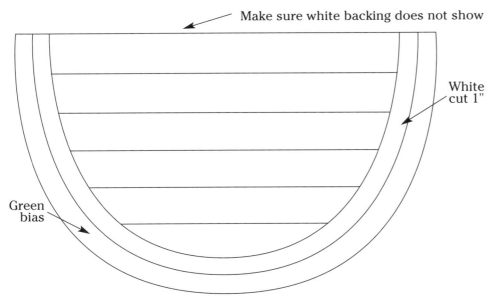

Make sure white backing does not show

White cut 1"

Green bias

Lazy Daisy Stitch

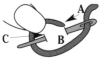

Come up at A. Go down at B (right next to A) to form a loop. Come back up at C with the needle tip over the thread. Go down at D to make a small anchor stitch over the top of the loop.

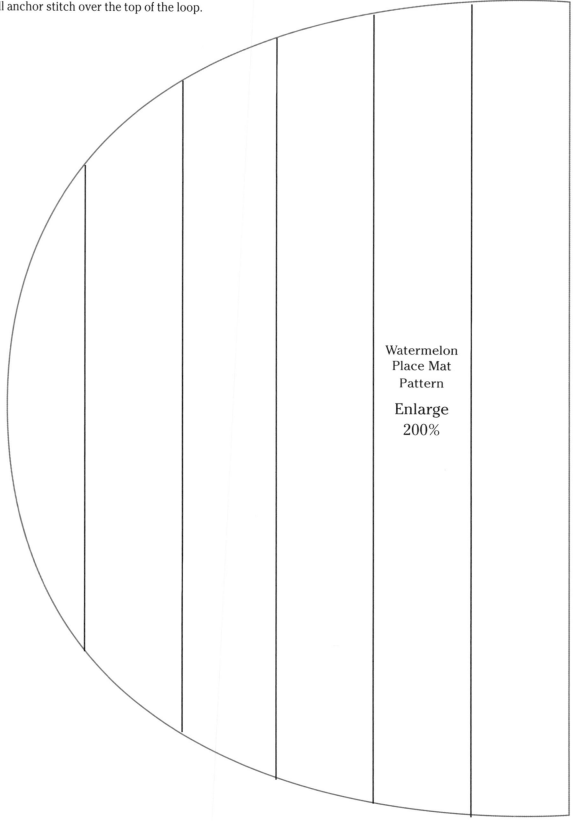

Watermelon
Place Mat
Pattern

**Enlarge
200%**

WALL HANGING:
30" x 37½"

PLACE MAT:
12" x 18"

'Hooray'
Wall Hanging and Place Mats

pattern by J. Jane Mitchell

pieced by Patsy Padgett

continued from pages 12 - 13

FINISHED BLOCK: 4⅞" x 6⅛"

Materials for Wall Hanging:

18 Blue 2½" x 41" strips (1¼ yds)

7 Red 2½" x 41" strips (½ yd)

8 Ecru 2½" x 41" strips (⅝ yd)

we used *Moda* 'Coming Home' collection

Backing material (1 yd)

Batting (32" x 40")

Binding (⅜ yd)

Paper piecing copies

Rotary cutter and mat

Fusible web

Clover Flower head pins (not necessary, but good to have)

Materials for One 8-Block Place Mat:

4 Blue 2½" x 41" strips (⅓ yd)

2 Red 2½" x 41" strips (¼ yd)

2 Ecru 2½" x 41" strips (¼ yd)

Batting 13" x 19"

Backing 13" x 19"

Binding (⅛ yd)

Fusible web

Wall Hanging Cutting Chart:

From Blue:

Cut 36 - 1¾" x 7" strips, 36 - 1¾" x 5½" strips, 36 - 1¾" x 3¾" strips, 36 - 1¾" x 2½" strips.

Set aside one of the Ecru strips (2½" x 41") for the 15 Ecru stars.

From Red and Ecru each:

Cut 7 strips in half lengthwise. Then subcut each color into 18 - 1¼" x 9", 18 - 1¼" x 7½", 18 - 1¼" x 6", 18 - 1¼" x 4½", 18 - 1¼" x 3".

This will make the 36 blocks needed for the wall hanging.

place mat Cutting Chart:

(makes one 8-block place mat):

Cut 3 Ecru stars out first.

Cut Blue:

Cut into 8 - 1¾" x 7", 8 - 1¾" x 5½", 8 - 1¾" x 3¾", 8 - 1¾" x 2½". Cut Red and Ecru in half lengthwise. Next subcut from each color 4 - 1¼" x 9", 4 - 1¼" x 7½", 4 - 1¼" x 6", 4 - 1¼" x 4½", 4 - 1¼" x 3".

This will make 8 blocks needed for 1 place mat.

Paper Piecing the Block:

Refer to the 'Log Cabin' Place Mats on page 71 for general instructions for paper piecing. You will need <u>9</u> copies <u>each</u> of blocks A, B, C, D.

NOTE: It is crucial that you sew exactly through the corners of the blocks. Otherwise, your points will not line up when you sew your blocks together.

On the pattern templates, there are corners that indicate that they may not be covered. If these corners are not covered with fabric, <u>don't panic</u>. Just be sure there is enough fabric to be caught by the next seam. Refer to paper piecing pattern on page 52 to see what I am explaining.

Block Placement and Piecing:

For the quilt you will need:

3 - CD units for Row 1   3 - AB units for Row 4

3 - AB units for Row 2   3 - CD units for Row 5

3 - CD units for Row 3   3 - AB units for Row 6

Sew right sides together   Sew right sides together

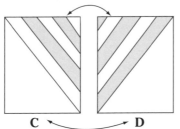
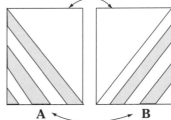

C   D   A   B

FYI: The Blue background seams from Row 1 are not supposed to line up with the Blue background seams from Row 2.

It will be <u>very easy</u> for you to get the blocks mixed up. Lay them out in front of you in the correct order and keep their letters attached to them. Letters will be reversed and patterns may be upside down because of paper piecing.

Just lay <u>finished</u> blocks out like first diagram.

Refer to the Wall Hanging photo for total placements.

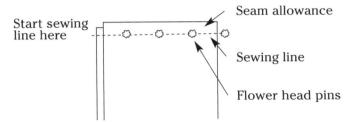

Start sewing line here

Seam allowance

Sewing line

Flower head pins

Here is a tip for joining the blocks and rows. This is where the *Clover* flower head pins come in handy. I use the pins that come in a package, not the ones that come in a box. The packaged ones have a thinner shaft.

<u>Match</u> the seam allowance on the paper pieces. Pin through the seam line front and back; the pins will lie flat. Shorten your stitch length to 1.50. Press seams <u>open</u>.

Begin sewing, removing the pins as you sew up to them one at a time.

This will keep your papers from shifting and will help in lining up your stripes and intersections. Join all blocks and rows in this same manner. Remove paper from seam allowances only before you sew over another seam. This will help avoid getting your paper stuck under the next seam.

When the <u>whole</u> top is completed, remove all the paper.

Applique the Stars:

After the whole top is pieced, you will need to applique the stars on.

Using fusible web, trace 15 stars. Cut them out outside the traced line.

Fuse them onto the <u>wrong</u> side of the Ecru strip you have set aside, following the manufacturer's instructions.

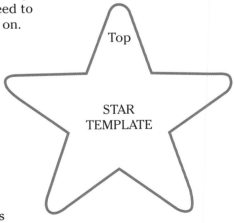

Top

STAR TEMPLATE

Cut stars out on the traced line. Remove paper backing. Five-pointed stars have a top and bottom, so be sure you lay them all out pointing up before you fuse them to the wall hanging.

If you prefer to hand-applique the stars, be sure to leave a scant ¼" around the star for turning under. I eyeballed the placement of the stars. Feel free to measure yours if it makes you more comfortable.

Sew down the fused stars using your favorite stitch.

Layering, Quilting, Binding and Hanging Sleeve:

You will find the instructions on how to layer, bind and make a hanging sleeve in the 'Birds in the Air' wall hanging on page 36.

Place Mats:

The place mats were quilted by machine. Here are two quilting options:

May we always be free. God bless our troops!

continued on pages 52 - 55

continued from pages 50 - 51

Corners that may not be covered

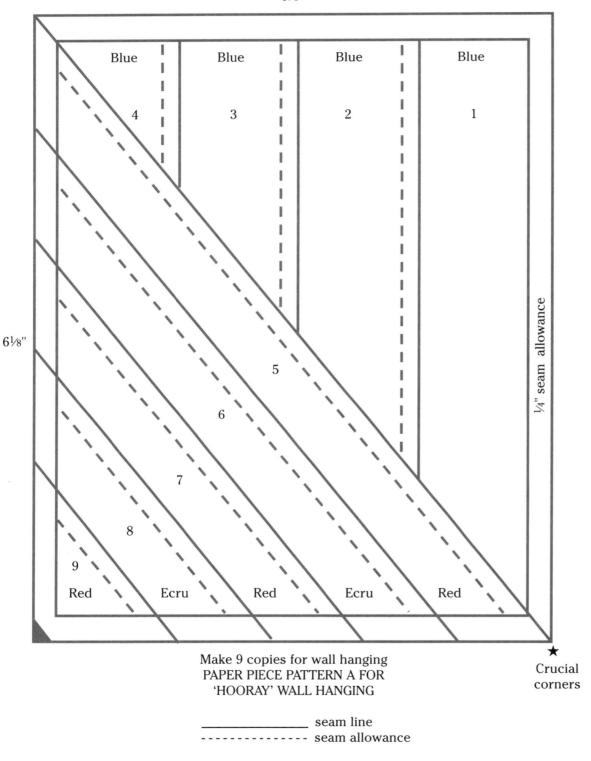

4⅞"

Blue

Blue

Blue

Blue

4

3

2

1

6⅛"

¼" seam allowance

5

6

7

8

9

Red   Ecru   Red   Ecru   Red

★

Crucial
corners

Make 9 copies for wall hanging
PAPER PIECE PATTERN A FOR
'HOORAY' WALL HANGING

_____ seam line
- - - - - - - - - - seam allowance

Make 2 copies for each place mat

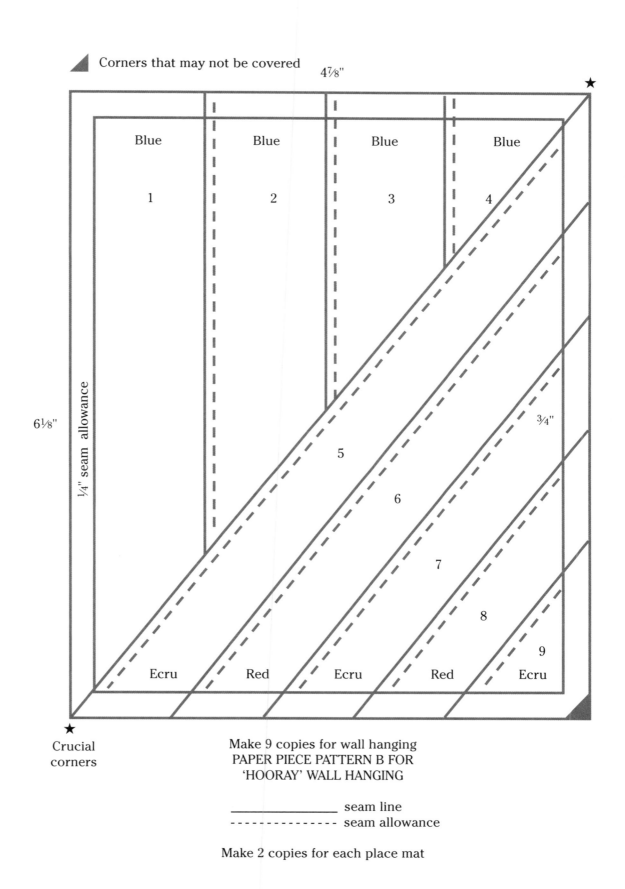

Corners that may not be covered

4⅞"

Blue 1　Blue 2　Blue 3　Blue 4

6⅛"

¼" seam allowance

5

6

¾"

7

8

9

Ecru　Red　Ecru　Red　Ecru

★ Crucial corners

Make 9 copies for wall hanging
PAPER PIECE PATTERN B FOR
'HOORAY' WALL HANGING

———————— seam line
- - - - - - - - - - - - - - seam allowance

Make 2 copies for each place mat

continued on pages 54 - 55

continued from pages 50 - 53

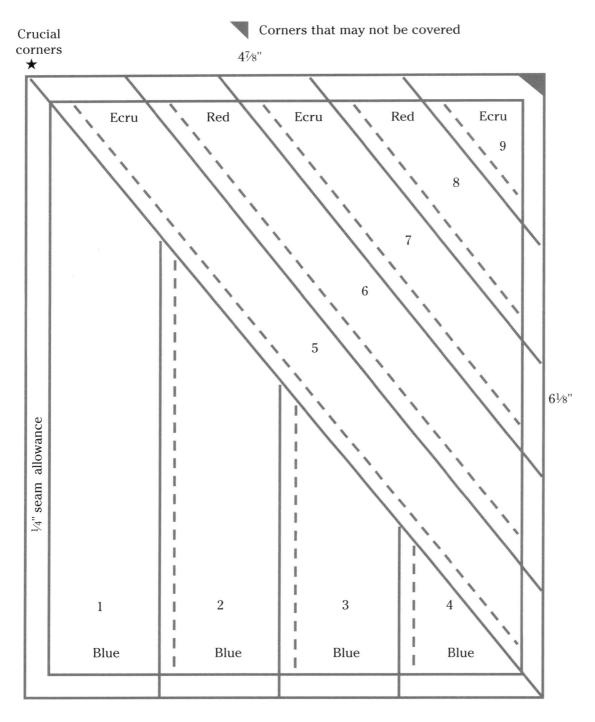

Crucial corners
★

Corners that may not be covered

4⅞"

Ecru   Red   Ecru   Red   Ecru

9

8

7

6

5

¼" seam allowance

6⅛"

1   2   3   4

Blue   Blue   Blue   Blue

Make 9 copies for wall hanging
PAPER PIECE PATTERN C FOR
'HOORAY' WALL HANGING

———————— seam line
- - - - - - - - - - - - seam allowance

Make 2 copies for each place mat

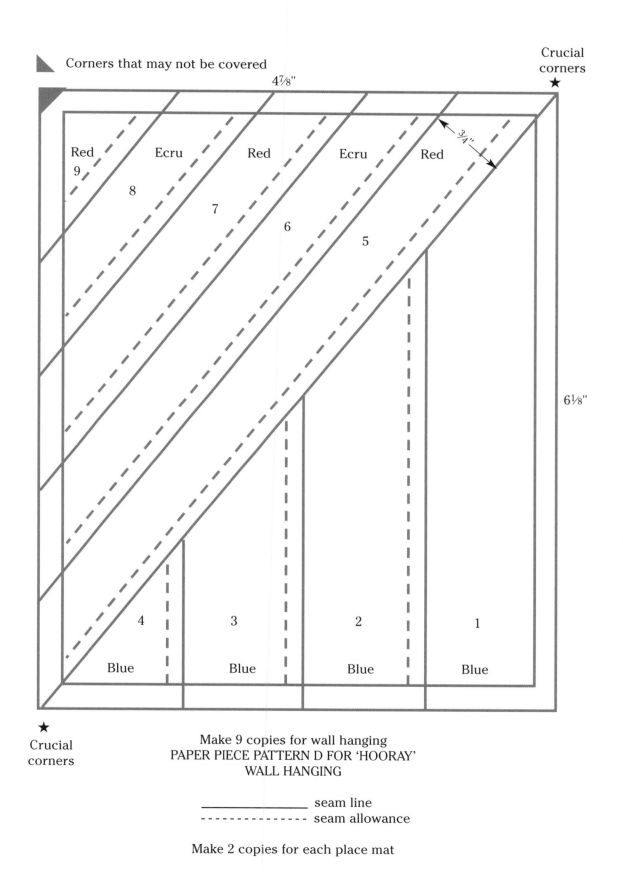

Corners that may not be covered

Crucial corners ★

4⅞"

Red 9

Ecru 8

Red 7

Ecru 6

Red 5

¾"

6⅛"

4

3

2

1

Blue

Blue

Blue

Blue

★
Crucial corners

Make 9 copies for wall hanging
PAPER PIECE PATTERN D FOR 'HOORAY'
WALL HANGING

————————— seam line
- - - - - - - - - - - - - seam allowance

Make 2 copies for each place mat

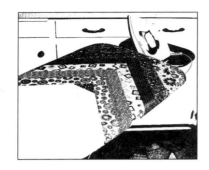

'Snappy' Ironing Board Cover

by Patsy Padgett

continued from page 14

SIZE: 21" x 56"

MATERIALS:

5 strips 2½" x 41" of Purple prints

3 strips 2½" x 41" of Aqua prints

> OR we used strips from a *Moda* 'Spring Fling'
> 'Jelly Roll' 2½" x 41" strips pack
> > (one pack is enough for more than two covers)

Fabric the length of your ironing board (Can be the silver silicon fabric or a nice weight cotton fabric)

Ruler with a 45 degree angle marking

Thread

Cord for drawstring

Assembly:

1. Remove your present ironing board cover.
2. Fold cover in half lengthwise. Press flat.
3. Place fold on the fold of your new fabric.
4. Cut new fabric ½" larger than original cover.
5. Unfold new fabric cover. Measure 17" from center

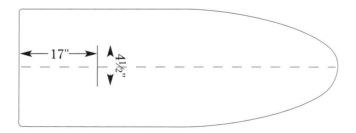

of widest end of cover and draw a centered line 4½" long.

> See diagram.

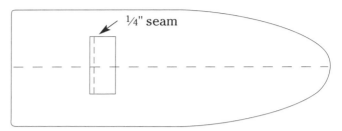

6. Cut a strip 2½" x 4½". Place right side of strip to the right side of cover with raw edge along marked 4½" line. Sew a ¼" seam. See diagram.

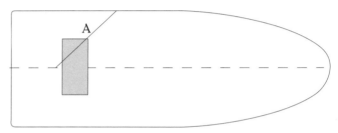

7. Flip and press.

8. Draw a 45 degree angle line crossing "A" from edge to center of cover. See diagram.

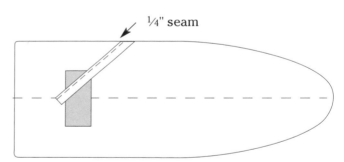

9. Place right side of 2½" strip to right side of cover with raw edge along the 45 degree angle line. Sew a ¼" seam from edge of cover to the center of cover. See diagram.

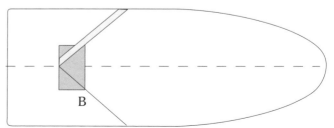

10. Flip and press.

11. Draw a 45 degree angle line crossing "B" from edge to center of cover. See diagram.

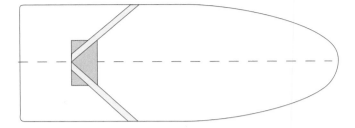

12. Place right side of 2½" strip to right side of cover along the 45 degree angle line just as you did the first strip. Sew a ¼" seam from edge of cover through previously flipped first strip. Trim the second strip along the end of the first strip.

13. Flip and press.

You have now completed the most important part of the construction process. The rest is fun, fun, fun!

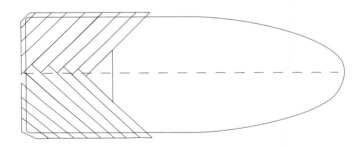

14. Lay next 2½" strip right sides together on the raw edge of first strip. Sew a ¼" seam. Flip and press.

15. Lay next 2½" strip right sides together on the raw edge of the second strip. Sew a ¼" strip seam. Trim, flip and press.

16. Repeat #14 and #15 until the end of the cover is completely covered with 2½" strips. See diagram.

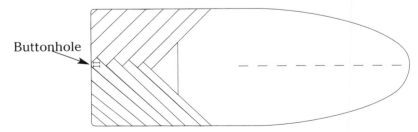

Buttonhole

17. Trim all edges of strips even with cover. Serge or zig-zag around edge of cover.

18. Make two small buttonholes close to center back edge of cover. These will be used to thread the drawstring through. See diagram.

19. Turn under and sew a ½" hem around the cover, easing in fullness on curves. Sew close to serged/zig-zagged edge as this is the casing for the drawstring.

20. Thread a drawstring with a bodkin through casing. Put a bead or a button on each end of drawstring.

21. Put your 'Snappy' Ironing Board Cover on your ironing board and enjoy!

NOTE: If you are making a smaller cover, make the 4½" line only 12" from end of board. Also, cut your 2½" strips in half.

SUGGESTION: If you need a new pad, just place a couple layers of batting on the back of your new cover and then serge or zig-zag through all layers before making your casing.

TIP: If you serge your edge, the casing isn't necessary. Your drawstring can be run through your serging stitches.

continued on pages 58 - 59

continued from pages 56 - 57

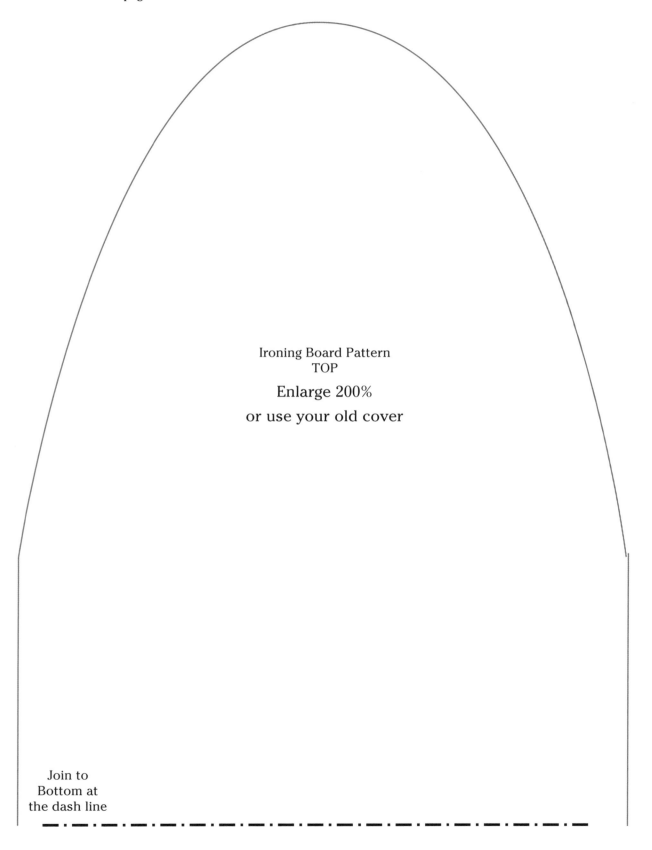

Ironing Board Pattern
TOP

Enlarge 200%

or use your old cover

Join to
Bottom at
the dash line

Join to
Top
at the
dash line

Ironing Board Pattern
BOTTOM
Enlarge 200%
or use your old cover

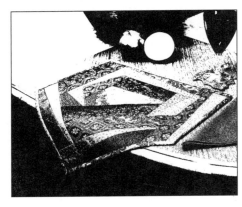

'Posy' Place Mat with Leaf Coaster

by J. Jane Mitchell

continued from page15

PLACE MAT: 18" x 19"

COASTER: 4¼" x 4¼"

Note: The technique is piecing on a foundation so that your place mat is quilted as you sew. When you are finished sewing, all you have to do is bind it.

Materials
for 1 Mat and 1 Coaster:

8 assorted Burgundy 2½" x 41"
     fabric strips:

Scrap of Yellow Gold 6" x 6"

Binding 2½" x 62"

Backing fabric 20" square

Scraps of 6 Green 6" x 6" squares
     for leaves and backing

Batting 20" square and 6" square

¼" sewing machine foot

Templastic material for making a
     leaf pattern

Black permanent marker

Copies of paper piecing

2" x 18" C-thru ruler
     (not necessary, but helpful)

Blue chalk marker

Red or Yellow chalk marker

Rotary cutter, mat and ruler

Place Mat Cutting Chart:
Yellow Golds:

   #1 - 2½" x 3½"; #2 - 2½" x 4"

Assorted Burgundies:

#3 - 2½" x 3½"
#4 - 2½" x 3½"
#5 - 2½" x 2½"
#6 - 2½" x 4½"
#6B - 2½" x 4½"
#7 - 2½" x 7½"
#7B - 2½" x 7½"
#8 - 2½" x 6½"
#8B - 2½" x 5½"
#9 - 2½" x 5½"
#9B - 2½" x 4½"
#10 - 2½" x 10"
#10B - 2½" x 9¼"
#11 - 2½" x 6"
#11B - 2½" x 5½"
#12 - 2½" x 11"
#12B - 2½" x 11"
#13 - 2½" x 9¼"
#13B - 2½" x 9"
#14 - 2½" x 10½"
#14B - 2½" x 9¼"
#15 - 2½" x 10¼"
#15B - 2½" x 9¼"
#16 - 2½" x 10¾"
#16B - 2½" x 10½"
#17 - 2½" x 12"
#17B - 2½" x 10½"

Leaf Coaster Cutting Chart:
Cut 5 assorted Greens into 1¼" strips

Constructing
the Coaster:

Take assorted Green 1¼" strips and paper piece leaf foundation. Instructions for paper piecing are found in 'Log Cabin' Place Mat instructions on page 71.

After you have made the leaf foundation, trace the leaf pattern onto templastic with a permanent marker.

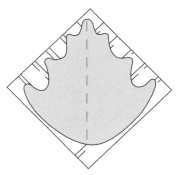

Cut the leaf out and place template onto leaf foundation. Trace around template directly on the wrong side of the leaf foundation, after the paper has been removed. Use a light hand to trace around the leaf so the ink will not bleed to the front side. This traced line will be the sewing line.

Layer batting <u>first</u>, backing <u>right</u> side up, then pieced leaf foundation <u>wrong</u> side up. Pin in place. Sew around the traced line, leaving about a 2½" opening at the bottom of the leaf foundation.

Trim to within ⅛" around the leaf (except at 2½" opening. Only trim the batting there, leaving ¼" of backing and top). Clip curves where needed.

Turn leaf right side out. Smooth seams and gently poke out leaf tips. Press. Handstitch opening closed. Add sewing machine stitch veins in leaf.

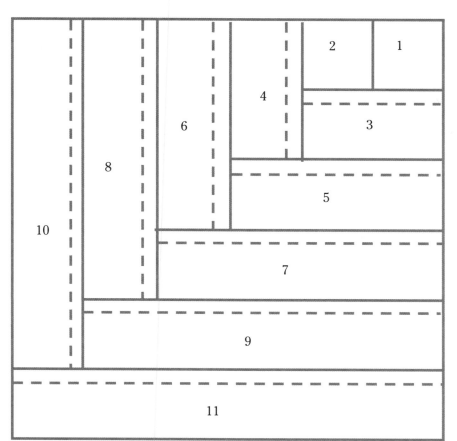

PAPER PIECING FOR LEAF COASTER

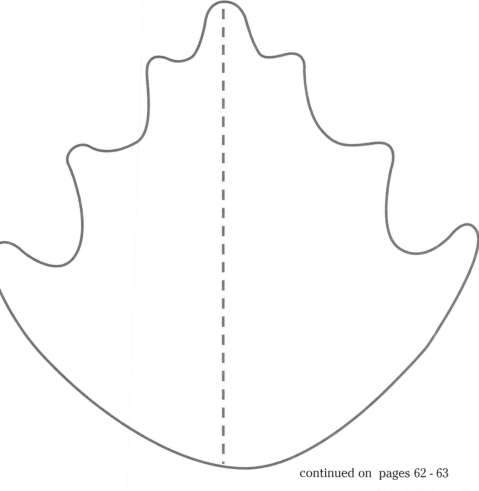

continued on pages 62 - 63

continued from pages 60 - 61

Constructing the Place Mat:

First mark the 20" square batting. Cut out place mat patterns, place it on your batting and trace around it with Blue chalk wheel.

Cut out batting on traced line. Mark ¼" seam allowance.

Now is where the 2" x 18" C-thru ruler comes in handy. Using it or a rotary ruler, mark a 2" line in from seam allowance line with a Blue chalk wheel in reverse numerical order starting with #17. Mark the #17B line. The #B's can be eyeballed.

Mark the #16 line, then the #16B line. Continue marking until the whole mat is marked finishing with #1.

All of the main numbers are 2" measurements.

All of the #B's are marked on an angle, inside the 2" measurement. When you get down to #5 through #1, don't worry about the size, but do be sure a 2½" strip will cover it.

Using a Red or Yellow chalk wheel, go back and mark the ¼" seam allowances on each # piece. Check the paper pattern to see which side to mark the allowance on.

When you have the whole piece marked with both seams and seam allowances, you are ready to layer, sew and quilt.

Sew and Quilt:

Lay the backing fabric right side <u>down</u>, place batting on top of backing, marked side <u>up</u>. Pin together in several places with straight pins.

Place #1 Yellow gold piece <u>right</u> side up on batting #1 area, lining it up with the (Yellow, Red) seam allowance marking between #1 and #2 batting area.

Place Yellow Gold #2 piece <u>right</u> side down on top of Yellow Gold #1 piece along seam allowance line. Sew a ¼" seam allowance (This is where you need your ¼" foot.) starting at the #10 sewing (Blue) line and stopping at the #7 sewing (Blue) line. Keep your paper pattern piece in front of you for easy reference.

Press Yellow Gold piece #2 open. Place Burgundy #3 piece <u>right</u> side down on top of Yellow Gold piece #2 and line it up to the seam allowance line in #3 area. If the seam allowance in the #3 space is covered by the Yellow Gold piece #2, trim the Yellow Gold piece back until you can see the seam allowance.

TIP: Fold fabric back over a scrap piece of templastic or cardstock and crease it. Cut along your crease with scissors.

Sew a ¼" seam starting at #10 Blue line and stopping at #4 Blue line. Press Burgundy #3 piece open. Next go on to Burgundy piece #4. You will continue in this manner until all of the areas are covered. Be sure that #12B, 13B, 15B, 16B and 17B cover the outside seam allowance.

Your place mat is now pieced <u>and</u> quilted, and only needs to be bound. On the sample, I took leftover 2½" assorted strips, cut them down to 2¼", and sewed them all together diagonally and used that for my binding. This helped to maintain the scrappy look.

Refer to the 'Log Cabin' Place Mats on page 71 for binding instructions.

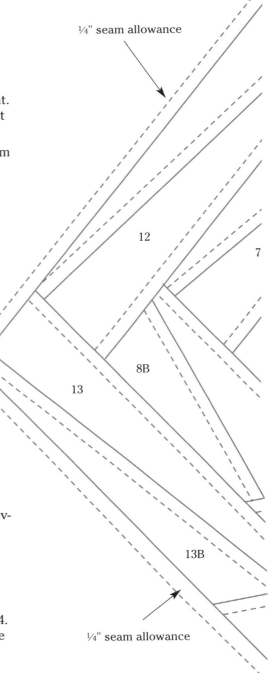

¼" seam allowance

12

7

8B

13

13B

¼" seam allowance

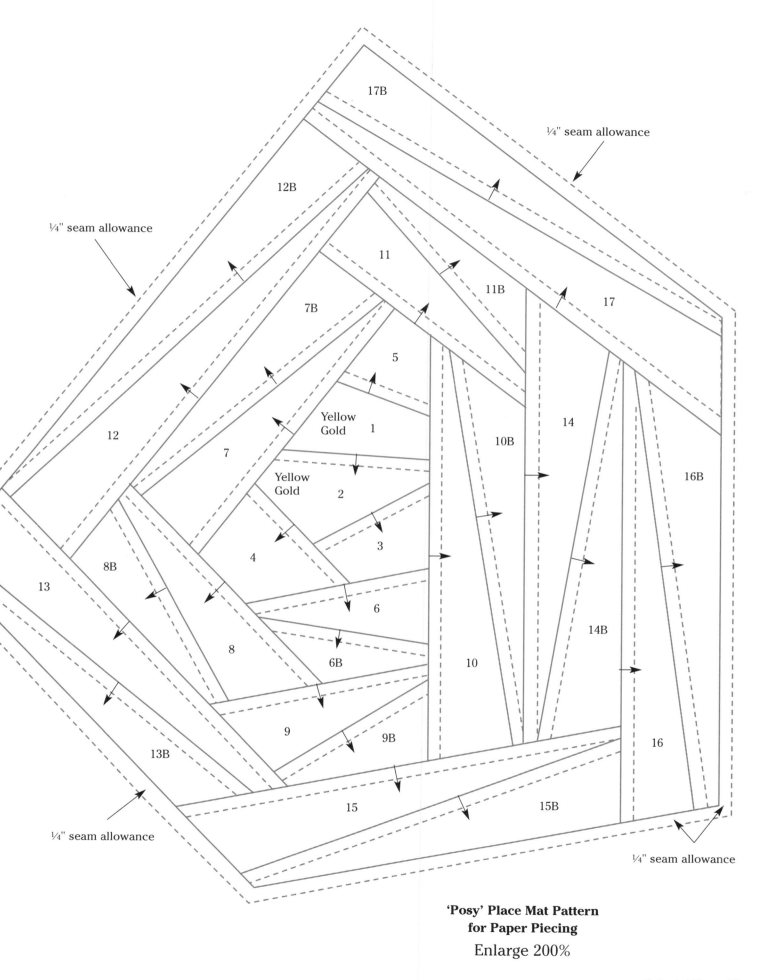

'Posy' Place Mat Pattern
for Paper Piecing
Enlarge 200%

Pumpkin' Table Topper

designed by J. Jane Mitchell

pieced by Patsy Padgett

continued from page 16

TABLE TOPPER: 21" x 37½"

FINISHED BLOCK: 9" x 9"

NOTE: If you prefer to paper piece, a pattern has been provided. You will need to make 12 copies of sub block, 4 copies of pumpkin and 4 copies of stem. See Paper Piecing instructions in 'Log Cabin' Place Mat instructions on page 71.

Materials:

2 strips (2½" x 41") <u>each</u> of 6 coordinating fabrics for square blocks (12 total)

1 strip of Light Orange

1 strip of Dark Orange

1 strip of Light Tan

1 strip of Dark Tan

3 strips of Black

    we used a *Moda* 'Serendipity' fat quarter collection

Scraps for stems - at least 6" square

⅔ yd backing fabric

⅔ yd x 42" batting

Rotary cutter, mat and ruler

Transparent template material

Black permanent marker

Fusible web

NOTE: ¼" seam allowances are used throughout this project (unless you choose to paper piece). Sew with right sides together.

Fabric Cutting Chart:

Remove selvages.

Cut 2 strips each out of the 6 coordinating color strips in half lengthwise. Subcut these strips into 12 - 1¼" x 5" strips of each color.

Light Orange: 2 - 2½" x 10½" strips; 4 - 2½" x 8¾" strips

Dark Orange: 4 - 2½" x 10½" strips; 4 - 1¼" x 5" strips

Light Tan: 2 - 2½" x 10½" strips; 4 - 2½" x 8¾" strips

Dark Tan: 4 - 2½" x 10½" strips; 4 - 1¼" x 5" strips

Black: 8 - 2½" x 4" strips (sides of pumpkin); 1 - 2½" x 16" strip (eyes and noses); 6 - 1¾" squares, then sub cut in half diagonally; 4 - 2½" x 6¼" strips (mouths)

Scraps: 4 - 1¼" squares for stems

Assembly of Coordinating Fabric Blocks:

This 9" block requires four 5" cut blocks (4½" finished sub blocks).

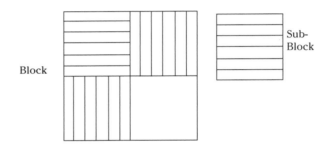

Lay 6 - 1¼" x 5" strips side by side in a pleasing color arrangement. Next sew the 6 strips right sides together, two at a time, using ¼" seam allowance. Wait to press them until all 6 strips have been sewn together. Press from the wrong side with all seam allowances going in the same direction. Turn over and press again on the right side. There is less distortion pressing them all at once. Press gently.

Square up the sub block to 5". If the sub block is way off size, check the seam allowances (¼") and the finished strip size (¾") and adjust accordingly. This step is very important. It ensures that when you sew the 4 sub blocks together you will have a 9½" cut block which finishes 9".

Make 11 more 5" sub blocks the same as the first one. For these next 11, it will be faster if you chain piece all your strips together. Chain piecing is when you sew the strips together without cutting the thread after each two strips are sewn.

EXAMPLE:

Then clip them apart and chain the next group together .

Just be sure that you are keeping them in the correct color order. Press in one direction after 6 strips have been sewn together.

Sew the 4 sub blocks together. They will form a plus sign in the middle.

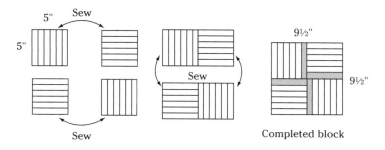

When you press the last seam, it will be necessary to clip it in the center so you can press it toward the least amount of bulk. It will be pressed in two directions.

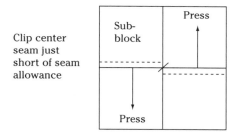

Check the completed block to be sure it measures 9½" unfinished. The pattern requires 3 of these blocks. When all 3 are completed, set them aside until later.

Assembly of the Four Pumpkin Blocks:

Starting with the middle 1¼" x 10½" Light Orange strip, sew a 2½" x 10½" Dark Orange strip to each side of middle strip.

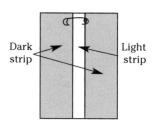

Press ¼" seams toward the narrower middle strip. Place a pin in the top of this to avoid confusion later on.

With right sides together sew Light Orange 2½" x 8¾" strips to each side of unit 1, offsetting them ¾" up from <u>bottom</u> of unit. Press.

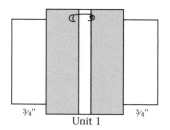

Sew 1¼" x 5" strips to both sides of pumpkin unit, offsetting them 1¾" up from <u>last sewn strip</u>. Press.

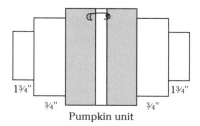

Sew Black 2½" x 4" strips to both sides of pumpkin unit, centering them with the last sewn strips. Press. Set aside.

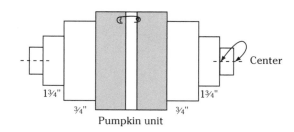

Make a template from the pumpkin diagram, including seam allowances and seam markings. Cut out template.

This will be your cutting line. Cut out on marked line. Set aside.

continued on pages 66 - 70

continued from pages 64 - 65

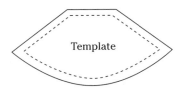

Place template over pumpkin unit, matching seam lines, and trace around it with a chalk or mechanical pencil. Be careful not to distort unit.

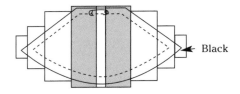

Assembly of Stem Unit:

Sew a Black half square triangle to the top of the stem unit. Press and trim dog ears off even with stem.

Sew a Black half square triangle to each side of stem unit, matching bottoms. Press seam allowance away from stem.

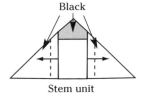

Place stem unit, right sides together, on pumpkin unit, matching seam lines of stem unit to seam lines of pumpkin unit. Sew. Press.

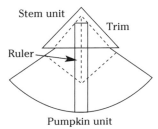

Take the corner of a 6" wide ruler, matching sides of pumpkin and trim stem unit to match pumpkin unit. You have just completed sewing one pumpkin. Make 1 more Orange pumpkin and 2 Tan pumpkins.

Eyes, Nose and Mouth:

Trace 8 eyes, 4 noses, and 4 mouths on fusible web. Cut out <u>outside</u> the traced pieces.

Fuse a mouth to each 2½" x 6¼" Black strip following manufacturer's instructions. Fuse the eyes and noses to the 2½" x 6¼" Black strip. Cut out on the traced lines and fuse to the pumpkins, using the diagram for placement.

Sew around the fused pieces with a blanket stitch, blind hem stitch or satin stitch. If you prefer to hand-applique, be sure to add a narrow seam turn-under to the pattern piece, rather than cutting out on the traced line (and of course you would eliminate the fusing process).

Assembling the Table Topper:

Lay out the 3 square blocks and 4 pumpkin blocks. Assemble the table topper in 3 diagonal rows, pressing toward the pumpkins.

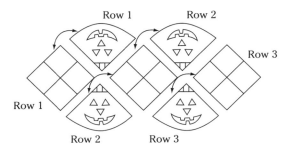

Sew the 3 rows together, matching up stem seams.

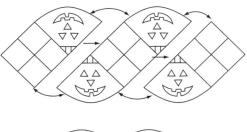

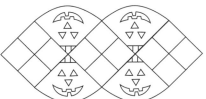

Layer the topper with batting. Place batting down first. Put backing with <u>wrong</u> side down onto batting. Place top <u>right</u> side down on backing. Pin in place. Sew around the outside edge using a ¼" seam allowance. Leave the topper open about 4" along one of the straight edges.

Paper piece pattern for Sub Block of 'Pumpkin' Table Topper. Make 12 copies. Sew in numerical order. Place fabric on back of paper. Sew on lines on front of paper. *Your color choices will be reversed. Allow for this in your placements.

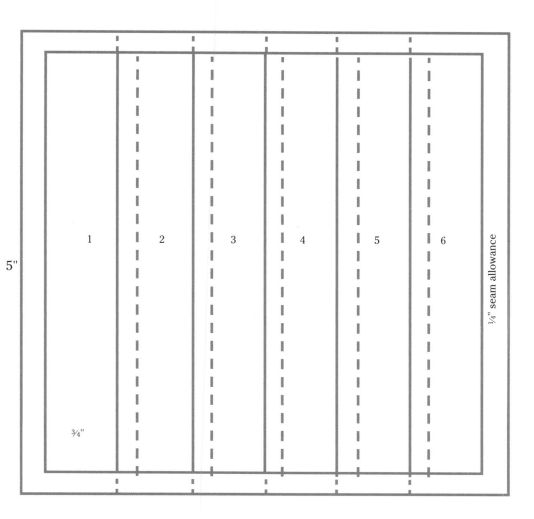

5"

1   2   3   4   5   6

¼" seam allowance

¾"

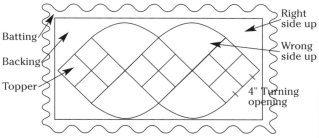

Batting

Backing

Topper

Right side up

Wrong side up

4" Turning opening

Trim around outside to a scant ¼" seam (except turning 4" - leave a full ¼" seam). Clip off tips. Turn through opening, smooth inside seam and push out points. Press. Slipstitch opening closed by hand.

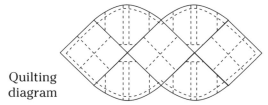

Quilting diagram

Quilt by hand or machine. The sample was quilted by machine 'in the ditch' using a straight stitch and a walking foot.

Depending on the size of your table, you may want to add more squares and pumpkins. Adjust fabric chart accordingly.

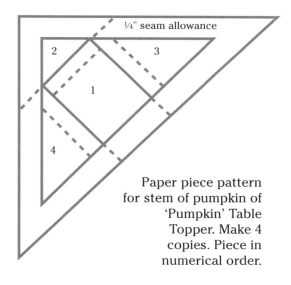

¼" seam allowance

2   3

1

4

Paper piece pattern for stem of pumpkin of 'Pumpkin' Table Topper. Make 4 copies. Piece in numerical order.

continued on pages 68 -70

continued from pages 64 - 67

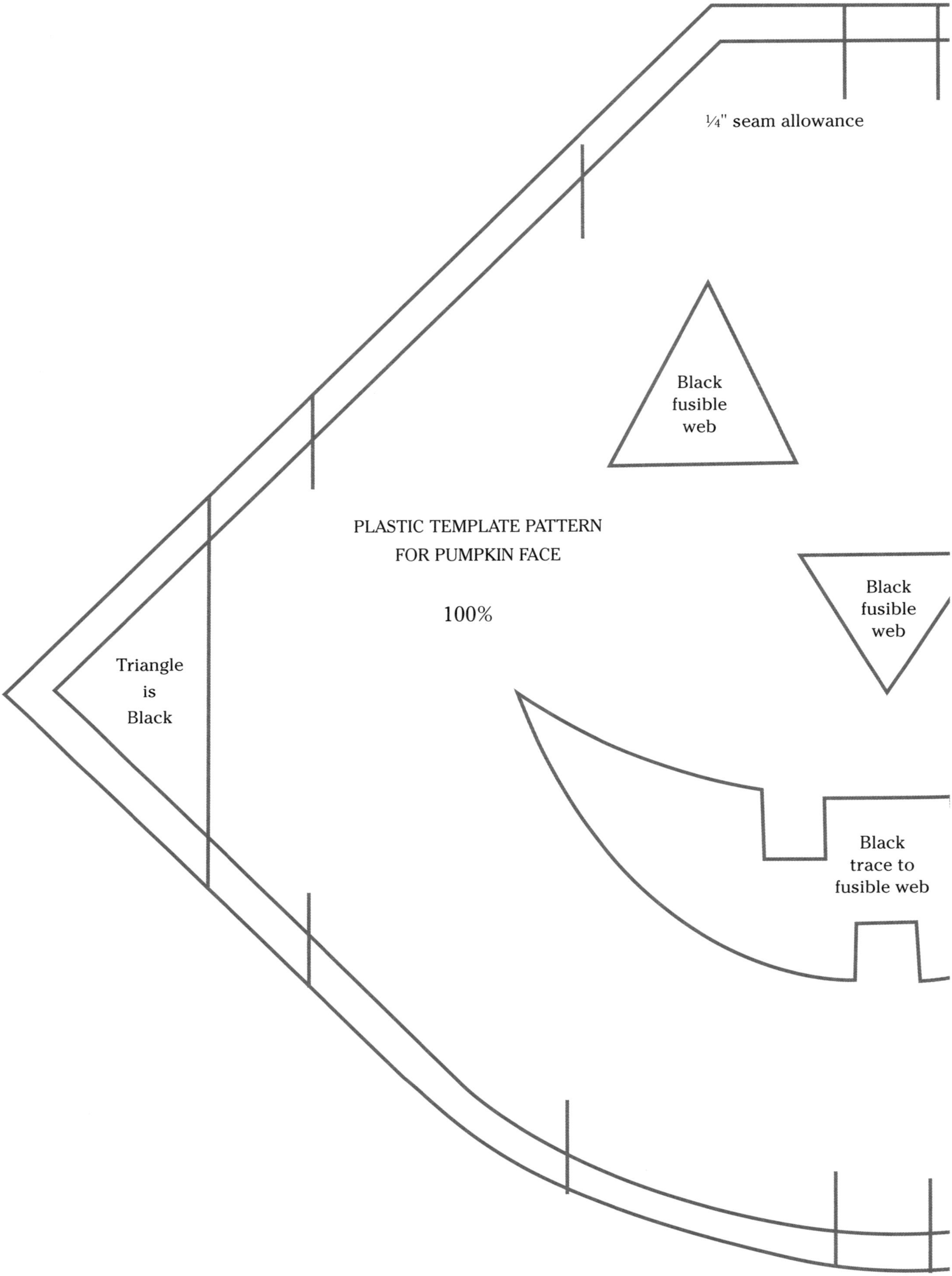

¼" seam allowance

Black
fusible
web

PLASTIC TEMPLATE PATTERN
FOR PUMPKIN FACE

100%

Black
fusible
web

Triangle
is
Black

Black
trace to
fusible web

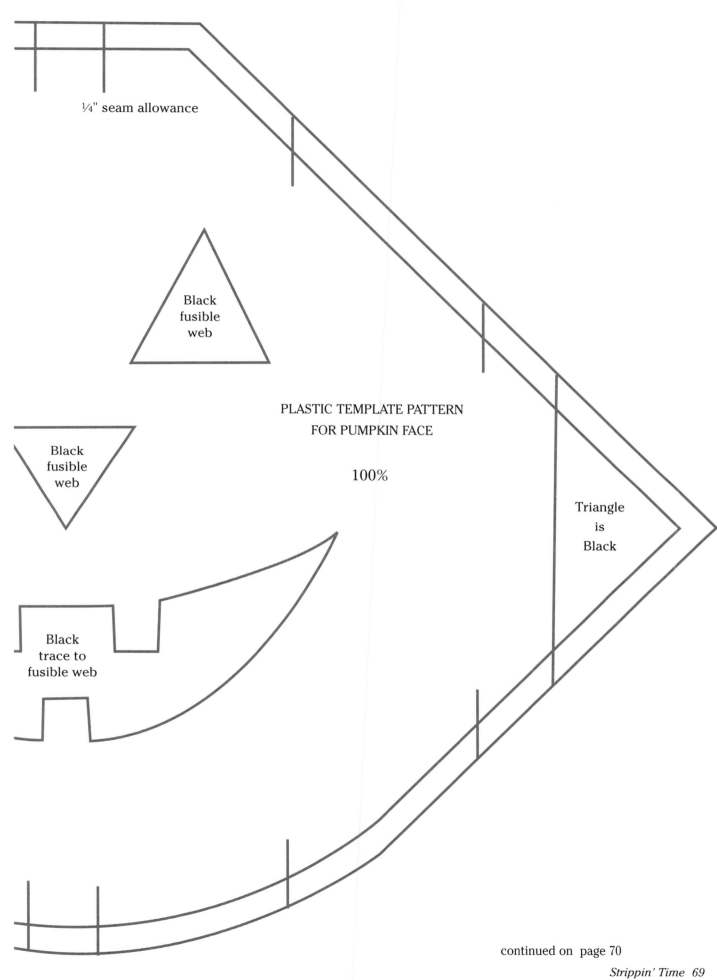

¼" seam allowance

Black fusible web

Black fusible web

Black trace to fusible web

PLASTIC TEMPLATE PATTERN
FOR PUMPKIN FACE

100%

Triangle is Black

continued on page 70

continued from pages 64 - 69

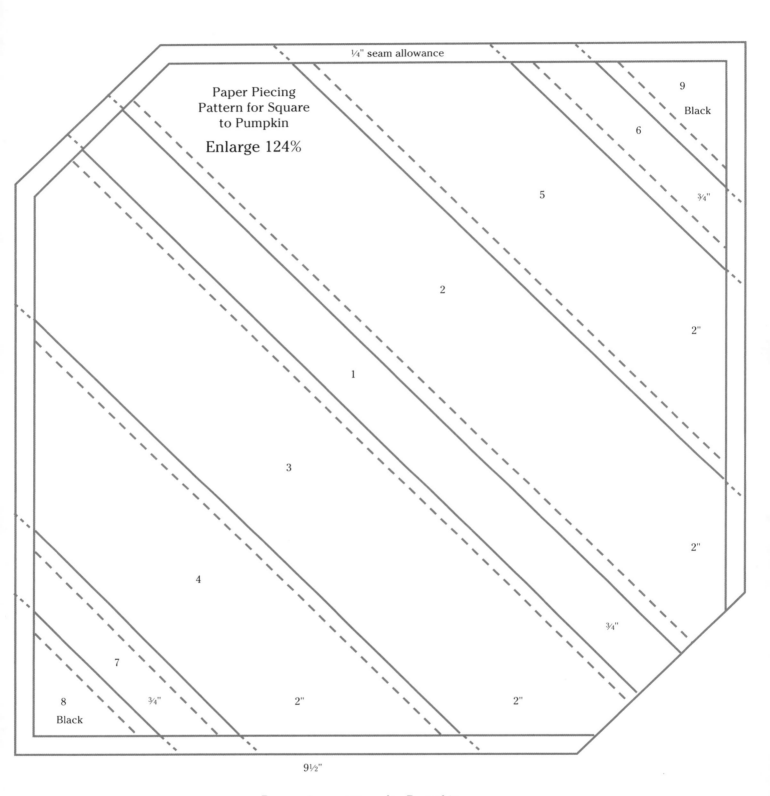

¼" seam allowance

Paper Piecing
Pattern for Square
to Pumpkin

Enlarge 124%

9

Black

6

5

¾"

2

2"

1

3

2"

4

¾"

7

8

Black

¾"

2"

2"

9½"

Paper piece pattern for Pumpkin
of 'Pumpkin' Table Topper. Make
4 copies. Sew in numerical order.

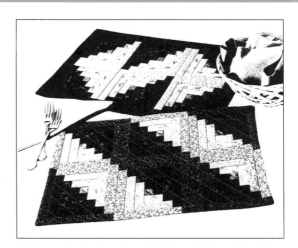

Cutting the Fabric Strips:

Remove selvages from strips.

Note: You will have enough leftover fabric from some of these strips to make part of another mat. Cut <u>enough</u> of these strips <u>in</u> <u>half</u> <u>lengthwise</u> to cut the following:

Gold: (#1) 6 - 1¼" x 1¼"

    Light Blue: (#2 & #3)
    6 - 1¼" x 1¼"; 6 - 1¼" x 2"

    Light Tan: (#4 & #5)
    6 - 1¼" x 2"; 6 - 1¼" x 2¾"

    Medium Blue: (#6 & #7)
    6 - 1¼" x 2¾"; 6 - 1¼" x 3½"

    Medium Tan: (#8 & #9)
     6 - 1¼" x 3½"; 6 - 1¼" x 4¼"

    Medium Dark Blue: (#10 & #11)
    6 - 1¼" x 4¼"; 6 - 1¼" x 5"

    Dark Tan: (#12 & #13)
    6 - 1¼" x 5"; 6 - 1¼" x 5¾"

    Dark Blue: (#14 & #15)
    6 - 1¼" x 5¾"; 6 - 1¼" x 6½"

This will make <u>one</u> place mat. Adjust fabric requirements by the number of place mats you wish to make.

'Log Cabin' Place Mats

pattern by J. Jane Mitchell

pieced by Patsy Padgett

continued from page 17

PLACE MAT: 12" x 18"

FINISHED BLOCK: 6" x 6"

MATERIALS FOR 1 MAT (BLUE & TAN):

8 strips (2½" x 41") of coordinating fabric:

    1 strips of GOLD

    1 strip <u>each</u> of Light, Medium & Dark Tan

    1 strip <u>each</u> of Light, Medium, Medium Dark & Dark Blue

    2 strips of Dark Blue for binding

    we used strips from a *Moda* 'Bound to the Prairie II' 'Jelly Roll' pack

13" x 19" backing

14" x 20" batting

6 paper piecing copies

Rotary cutter, mat, ruler

Assembling Blocks:

To make the best use of the 'jelly roll' strips, you will have to use a <u>scant</u> ¼" seam allowance when paper piecing.

The seam allowance on the paper piecing pattern are the dashed lines.

The sewing lines are the solid lines.

continued on pages 72 - 76

continued from pages 74 - 76

A Word About Paper Piecing:

Using paper to piece ensures that the blocks will be very accurate. You will piece in the numerical order printed on the pattern. Press after each sewn piece of fabric.

Tip: Shorten your stitch length for easy removal of paper (1.5). Do not remove the paper until all 6 blocks are completed.

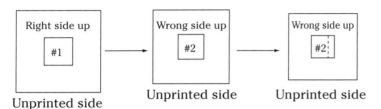

Start by sewing #2 to #1. Place #1 right side up (RSU) on the <u>unprinted</u> side of the pattern. Place #2 wrong side up (WSU) onto #1.

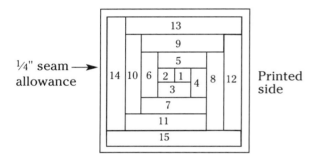

You will need to use a light source, such as a window or a lamp, and hold the block up to see the shadows on the fabric to be sure they are placed correctly over the seam allowance (the dashed lines).

Use a pin to hold the fabrics in place.

Turn the block over to the <u>printed</u> side and sew on the solid line between #1 and #2.

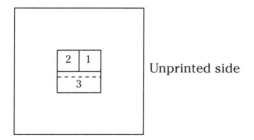

After sewing flip block over to unprinted side and press seam open with a dry iron.

Hold block up to light source and check to see that piece #2 will cover the #2 area plus the scant ¼" seam allowance in the #3 area.

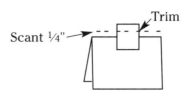

If it is more than a scant ¼" seam, fold the paper toward you on the just sewn seam line and trim fabric down to ¼" scant seam allowance.

If it does not cover the scant ¼" seam allowance on the #2 area, you will need to adjust it and resew it. Once you have mastered the first seam, move on to piece #3. Continue adding strips in numerical order to the unprinted side of pattern, right sides together.

Pin and sew on the printed side of the pattern. Always check to be sure the seam allowance of the next area is covered. Press after each strip is sewn. Strips #12, 13, 14, and 15 must cover the <u>full</u> ¼" seam allowances around the outside edges.

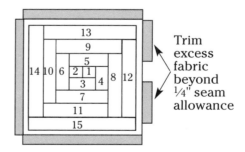

The fabric is <u>right</u> side up on the <u>unprinted</u> side of the pattern when you are finished sewing. This will seem backwards to you, but you will soon get the hang of it.

After you have sewn all of the 15 strips to the pattern, turn it over to the printed side and trim around the <u>outside</u> line of the block. <u>Make sure</u> to leave a <u>full</u> ¼" seam allowance on all 4 sides. You are just cleaning up any fabric overhang that you may have.

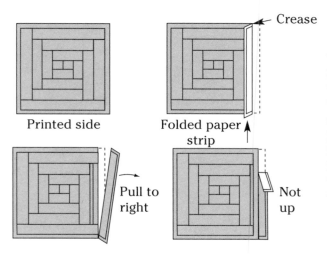

Printed side

Folded paper strip

Crease

Pull to right

Not up

Construct the next 5 blocks in the same manner. Now you may remove the paper pattern. To do this, fold the paper of #15 strip toward you and crease it on the sewing line. when you tear the paper off, do <u>not</u> tear it <u>up</u>, but rather <u>pull</u> it to the right, away from the last seam. This will prevent damaging the seam and distorting the block.

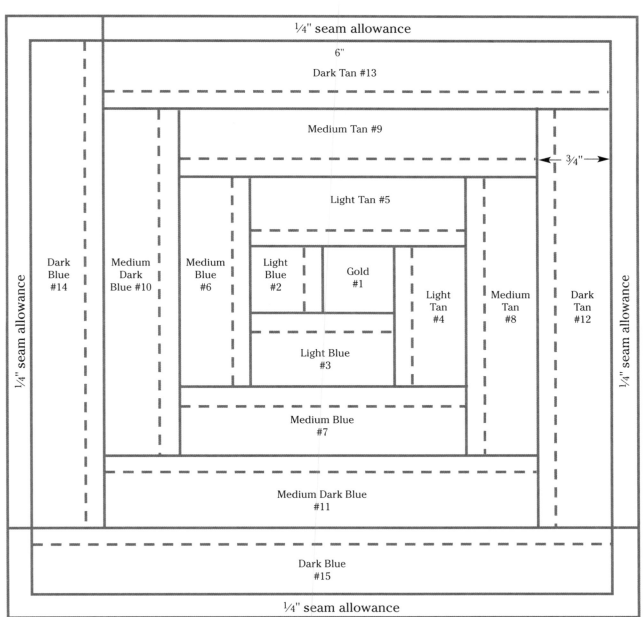

¼" seam allowance

6"

Dark Tan #13

Medium Tan #9

¾"

Light Tan #5

Dark Blue #14

Medium Dark Blue #10

Medium Blue #6

Light Blue #2

Gold #1

Light Tan #4

Medium Tan #8

Dark Tan #12

¼" seam allowance

¼" seam allowance

Light Blue #3

Medium Blue #7

Medium Dark Blue #11

Dark Blue #15

¼" seam allowance

Piece in numerical order. If you find that your strips are not covering the next space, make your seam allowances narrower.

———————— sewing line

- - - - - - - - - - seam allowance

continued on pages 74 - 76

continued from pages 70 - 73

Sew   Sew

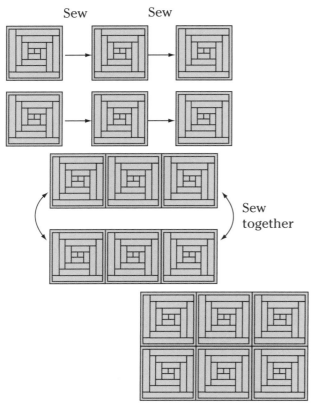

If some of the paper is caught under a seam, a pair of sharp tweezers is helpful to dislodge any small scraps.

Lay the 6 blocks in front of you, turning them until you get a design that you like. Refer to place mat photo to see two examples of designs you can make. When you have the desired design, sew the blocks right sides together.

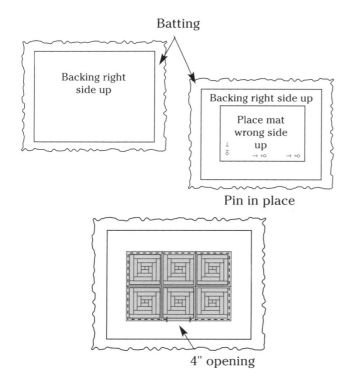

Options for Finishing:

Option 1:

Unbound and turned. Lay the batting (14" x 20") out in front of you. Place the backing (13" x 19") on top of the batting <u>right</u> side up.

Place the place mat <u>wrong</u> side up on top of backing. Pin in place.

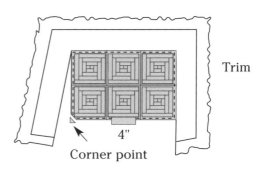

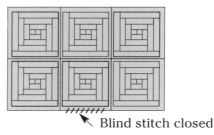

Sew around layered place mat ¼" seam allowance leaving about 4" open on one side for turning.

After sewing, trim backing, batting and place mat to a scant ¼" seam except for 4" turning opening. Leave a full ¼" seam allowance here so you can hand sew it shut.

Trim off the 4 corner points.

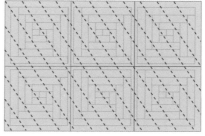

Turn through 4" opening. Poke out 4 corners and smooth out around all 4 seams. Press. Turn ¼" seam allowance inside of mat at the 4" opening and close opening by hand with a blind stitch.

Your place mat is now ready for quilting, either by hand or machine. The Burgundy place mat was finished with this option and quilted by machine. The quilting lines are approximately 1" apart and then quilted inside the last 4 strips, giving the illusion of a binding.

Option 2:

Bound. Layer the mat in this order: Backing <u>right</u> side down. Place batting on top of backing. Place mat <u>right</u> side up on top of batting. Pin in place. Quilt by hand or machine.

The Navy Blue place mat was quilted by machine 'in the ditch' (along the seam lines) to form squares.

You will need 2 strips (2½" x 41") or a strip of backing fabric that is 2½" x 68". Remove the selvages. Sew 2 strips together diagonally with right sides together as shown in Diagram A.

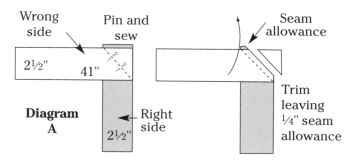

Diagram A

Trim leaving a ¼" seam allowance.

Press strip open and press open seam allowance. Fold the long strip in half lengthwise, wrong sides together.

This will give you a 1¼" wide folded binding strip. Place this strip on top of the right side of the place mat, lining up raw edges of strip to raw edges of place mat.

Using a ¼" seam allowance, begin sewing the strip about 6" from the end of the strip.

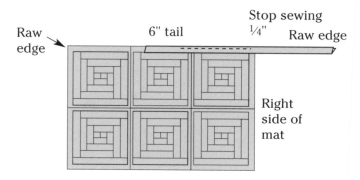

When you come to the corner, stop sewing ¼" from the edge of the place mat.

Remove the place mat from sewing machine. Lift binding straight up parallel with the right edge of the place mat (Diagram B).

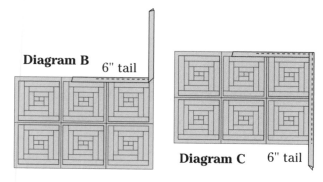

Diagram B 6" tail

Diagram C 6" tail

Fold it back down even with the top of the place mat (Diagram C). With a ¼" seam allowance, begin sewing down the right side of the place mat. Stop ¼" from bottom edge of place mat. Remove place mat from machine.

Turn place mat counterclockwise. Lift binding to the top of the place mat (Diagram D) and then back down again (Diagram E) as you did with the last corner.

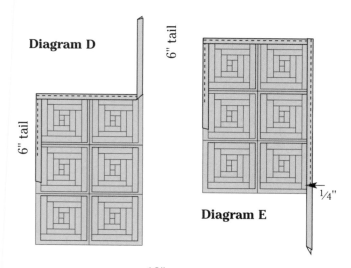

Diagram D

6" tail

6" tail

Diagram E

¼"

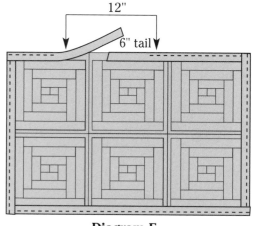

12"

6" tail

Diagram E

Continue around the place mat until you have completed all 4 corners.

Stop sewing the binding about 12" from where you started sewing the binding (Diagram F). Remove place mat from machine.

continued on page 76

continued from pages 70 - 75

How to Join Binding Ends Diagonally:

Lay place mat right side up in front of you, with the unsewn binding at the top of the mat.

Overlap the end of the binding strip on the beginning binding strip the width of the unfolded binding and cut off.

In this case it is 2½". (Diagram G)

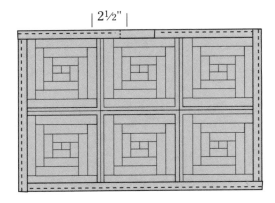

Diagram G

Open the 1¼" folds so that they are 2½" again. Overlap them at right angles and place right sides together.

Pin and draw a diagonal line through the pinned area (Diagram H).

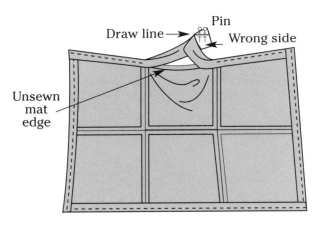

Diagram H

Sew the ends together along marked line. Do not cut yet. Gently refold the binding back in half (1¼") and lay it on top of the unsewn part of the mat. If you have measured and sewn correctly, it should fit perfectly. Now you can open it back up and trim a ¼" seam allowance (Diagram I).

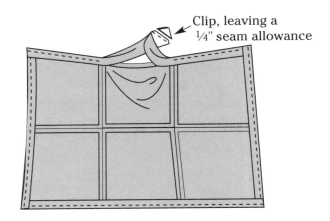

Diagram I

Finger press the ¼" seam allowance open.

Refold it and lay it back on top of your place mat and finish sewing the binding on (Diagram J).

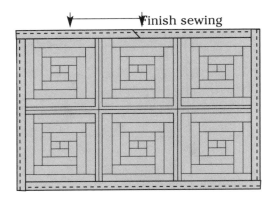

Diagram J

Trim the backing and the batting a generous ¼" in from the sewing line of the binding. This will ensure that your binding will not end up void of batting.

Fold the binding to the back of the place mat and handstitch it down along the stitch line created when you machine sewed the binding to the front of the place mat.

You have completed one place mat. Congratulations!

NOTE: If you feel real ambitious, you could piece 2 place mat tops of contrasting colors. Use one for the backing and the other for the front to have reversible place mats. Neat idea!

Bon appetit!

Basic Cutting Instructions

Tips for Accurate Cutting:
Accurate cutting is easy when using a rotary cutter with a sharp blade, a cutting mat, and a transparent ruler. Begin by pressing your fabric and then follow these steps:

1. Folding:
a) Fold the fabric with the selvage edges together. Smooth the fabric flat. If needed, fold again to make your fabric length smaller than the length of the ruler.

b) Align the fold with one of the guide lines on the mat. This is important to avoid getting a kink in your strip.

2. Cutting:
a) Align the ruler with a guide line on the mat. Press down on the ruler to prevent it shifting or have someone help hold the ruler. Hold the rotary cutter along the edge of the ruler and cut off the selvage edge.

b) Also using the guide line on the mat, cut the ends straight.

c) Strips for making the quilt top may be cut on the crosswise grain (from selvage to selvage) or on grain (parallel to the selvage edge). Strips for borders should be cut on grain (parallel to the selvage edge) to prevent wavy edges and make quilting easier.

d) When cutting strips, move the ruler, NOT the fabric.

Basic Sewing Instructions

You now have precisely cut strips that are exactly the correct width. You are well on your way to blocks that fit together perfectly. Accurate sewing is the next important step.

Matching Edges:
1. Carefully line up the edges of your strips. Many times, if the underside is off a little, your seam will be off by ⅛". This does not sound like much until you have 8 seams in a block, each off by ⅛". Now your finished block is a whole inch wrong!
2. Pin the pieces together to prevent them shifting.

Seam Allowance:
I cannot stress enough the importance of accurate ¼" seams. All the quilts in this book are measured for ¼" seams unless otherwise indicated.

Most sewing machine manufacturers offer a Quarter-inch foot. A Quarter-inch foot is the most worthwhile investment you can make in your quilting.

Pressing:
I want to talk about pressing even before we get to sewing because proper pressing can make the difference between a quilt that wins a ribbon at the quilt show and one that does not.

Press, do NOT iron. What does that mean? Many of us want to move the iron back and forth along the seam. This "ironing" stretches the strip out of shape and creates errors that accumulate as the quilt is constructed. Believe it or not, there is a correct way to press your seams, and here it is:

1. Do not use steam with your iron. If you need a little water, spritz it on.
2. Place your fabric flat on the ironing board without opening the seam. Set a hot iron on the seam and count to 3. Lift the iron and move to the next position along the seam. Repeat until the entire seam is pressed. This sets and sinks the threads into the fabric.
3. Now, carefully lift the top strip and fold it away from you so the seam is on one side. Usually the seam is pressed toward the darker fabric, but often the direction of the seam is determined by the piecing requirements that will come later.
4. Press the seam open with your fingers. Add a little water or spray starch if it wants to close again. Lift the iron and place it on the seam. Count to 3. Lift the iron again and continue until the seam is pressed. Do NOT use the tip of the iron to push the seam open. So many people do this and wonder later why their blocks are not fitting together.
5. Most critical of all: Every seam must be pressed before the next seam is sewn.

Working with Crosswise Grain strips:
Strips cut on the crosswise grain (from selvage to selvage) have problems similar to bias edges and are prone to stretching. To reduce stretching and make your quilt lay flat for quilting, keep these tips in mind.
1. Take care not to stretch the strips as you sew.
2. Adjust the sewing thread tension and the presser foot pressure if needed.
3. If you detect any puckering as you go, rip out the seam and sew it again. It is much easier to take out a seam now than to do it after the block is sewn.

Sewing Bias Edges:
Bias edges wiggle and stretch out of shape very easily. They are not recommended for beginners, but even a novice can accomplish bias edges if these techniques are employed.
1. Stabilize the bias edge with one of these methods:
a) Press with spray starch.
b) Press freezer paper or removable iron-on stabilizer to the back of the fabric.
c) Sew a double row of stay stitches along the bias edge and ⅛" from the bias edge. This is a favorite technique of garment makers.
2. Pin, pin, pin! I know many of us dislike pinning, but when working with bias edges, pinning makes the difference between intersections that match and those that do not.

Building Better Borders:
Wiggly borders make a quilt very difficult to finish. However, wiggly borders can be avoided with these techniques.
1. Cut the borders on grain. That means cutting your strips parallel to the selvage edge.
2. Accurately cut your borders to the exact measure of the quilt.
3. If your borders are piece stripped from crosswise grain fabrics, press well with spray starch and sew a double row of stay stitches along the outside edge to maintain the original shape and prevent stretching.
4. Pin the border to the quilt, taking care not to stretch the quilt top to make it fit. Pinning reduces slipping and stretching.

Tips for Working with Strips

Pre-cut strips are cut on the crosswise grain and are prone to stretching. These tips will help reduce stretching and make your quilt lay flat for quilting.

1. If you are cutting yardage, cut on the grain. Cut fat quarters on grain, parallel to the 18" side.

2. When sewing crosswise grain strips together, take care not to stretch the strips. If you detect any puckering as you go, rip out the seam and sew it again.

3. Press, Do Not Iron. Carefully open fabric, with the seam to one side, press without moving the iron. A back-and-forth ironing motion stretches the fabric.

4. Reduce the wiggle in your borders with this technique from garment making. First, accurately cut your borders to the exact measure of the quilt top. Then, before sewing the border to the quilt, run a double row of stay stitches along the outside edge to maintain the original shape and prevent stretching. Pin the border to the quilt, taking care not to stretch the quilt top to make it fit. Pinning reduces slipping and stretching.

Basic Iron-On Applique Instructions

Using Fusible Web:

1. Trace the pattern onto fusible web and cut out.

2. Press the patterns onto the wrong side of the fabric.

3. Cut out patterns exactly on the drawn line.

4. Score the web paper with a pin to remove the paper.

5. Position the fabric, fusible side down, on the quilt and press with a hot iron following the fusible web manufacturer's instructions. Different brands require different heating times.

6. Stabilize the wrong side of the fabric with your favorite stabilizer.

7. Use a size 80 machine embroidery needle. Fill the bobbin with lightweight basting thread and thread the machine with a machine embroidery thread that complements the color being appliqued.

8. Set your machine for a Zigzag stitch and adjust the thread tension if needed. Use a scrap to experiment with different stitch widths and lengths until you find the one you like best.

9. Sew slowly.

Basic Layering Instructions

Marking Your Quilt:

If you choose to mark your quilt for hand or machine quilting, it is much easier to do so before layering. Press your quilt before you begin. Here are some handy tips regarding marking.
1. Disappearing pen may vanish before you finish.
2. Use a White pencil on dark fabrics.
3. If using a washable Blue pen, remember that pressing will make the pen permanent.

Pieced Backings:
1. Press the backing fabric before measuring.
2. Cut backing fabrics on grain, parallel to the selvage edges.
3. Piece 3 parts rather than 2 whenever possible, sewing 2 side borders to the center. This reduces stress on the pieced seam.
4. The backing and batting should extend at least 2" on each side of the quilt.

Creating a Quilt Sandwich:
1. Press the backing and top to remove all wrinkles.
2. Lay the backing wrong side up on the table.
3. Position the batting over the backing and smooth out all wrinkles.
4. Center the quilt top over the batting leaving a 2" border all around.
5. Pin the layers together with 2" safety pins positioned a handwidth apart. A grapefruit spoon makes inserting the pins easier. Leaving the pins open in the container speeds up the basting on the next quilt.

Basic Quilting Instructions

Hand Quilting:

Many quilters enjoy the serenity of hand quilting. Because the quilt is handled a great deal, it is important to securely baste the sandwich together. Place the quilt in the hoop and don't forget to hide your knots.

Machine Quilting:

All the quilts in this book were machine quilted. Some were quilted on a large, free-arm quilting machine and others were quilted on a sewing machine. If you have never machine quilted before, practice on some scraps first.

Straight Line Machine Quilting Tips:
1. Pin baste the layers securely.
2. Set up your sewing machine with a size 80 quilting needle and a walking foot.
3. Experimenting with the decorative stitches on your machine adds interest to your quilt. You do not have to quilt the entire piece with the same stitch. Variety is the spice of life, so have fun trying out stitches you have never used before as well as your favorite stand-bys.

Free Motion Machine Quilting Tips:
1. Pin baste the layers securely.
2. Set up your sewing machine with a spring needle, a quilting foot, and lower the feed dogs.

Basic Binding Instructions

A Perfect Finish:

The binding endures the most stress on a quilt and is usually the first thing to wear out. For this reason, we recommend using a double fold binding.

1. Trim the backing and batting even with the quilt edge.

2. Cut strips on the crosswise grain because a little bias in the binding is a Good thing. This is the only place in the quilt where bias is helpful, for it allows the binding to give as it is turned to the back and sewn in place.

3. Strips are usually cut 2½" wide, but check the instructions for your project before cutting.

4. Sew strips end to end diagonally to make a long strip sufficient to go all around the quilt plus 2"- 4".

5. With wrong sides together, fold the strip in half lengthwise. Press.

6. Stretch out your hand and place your little finger at the corner of the quilt top. Place the binding where your thumb touches the edge of the quilt. Aligning the edge of the quilt with the raw edges of the binding, pin the binding in place along the first side.

7. Leaving a 2" tail for later use, begin sewing the binding to the quilt with a ¼" seam.

8. Stop ¼" from the first corner. Leave the needle in the quilt and turn it 90°. Hit the reverse button on your machine and back off the quilt leaving the threads connected.

9. Fold the binding perpendicular to the side you sewed, making a 45° angle. Carefully maintaining the first fold, bring the binding back along the edge to be sewn.

10. Carefully align the edges of the binding with the quilt edge and sew as you did the first side. Repeat this process until you reach the tail left at the beginning. Fold tail out of the way, sew until you are ¼" from the beginning stitches.

11. Remove the quilt from the machine. Fold the quilt out of the way and match the binding tails together. Carefully sew the binding tails with a ¼" seam. You can do this by hand if you prefer.

12. Trim the seam to reduce bulk.

13. Finish stitching the binding to the quilt across the join you just sewed.

14. Turn the binding to the back of the quilt. To reduce bulk at the corners, fold the miter in the opposite direction from which it was folded on the front.

15. Hand sew a Blind stitch on the back of the quilt to secure the binding in place.

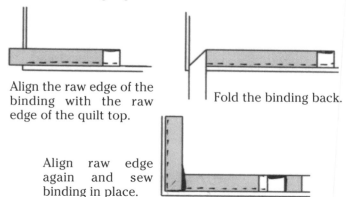

Align the raw edge of the binding with the raw edge of the quilt top.

Fold the binding back.

Align raw edge again and sew binding in place.

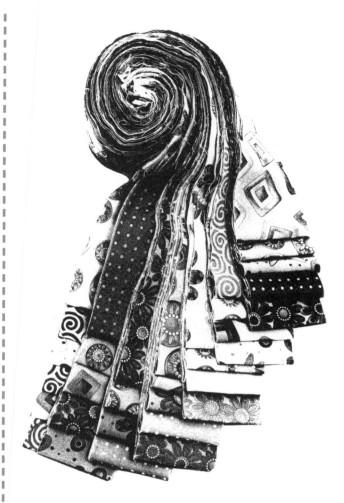

'Jelly Rolls'

Perfect Collections of Pre-cut Fabric Strips

'Jelly Rolls' are pre-cut collections of fabric, with every fabric cut to a 2½" wide x 40" long strip.

The strips are easy to use and because they are pre-cut, you can start sewing right away. If you prefer other colors of fabric, you can cut your own strips with a rotary cutter and mat.

The Best Things About

'Jelly Rolls'

Non-Fattening

Sugar Free

Fat Free

No Cholesterol

Friendship Pins

Friendship Pins

inspired by Susan Fuqua

pieced by Patsy Padgett

continued from page 83

SIZE: 2½" x 2½"

Note: These pins are made from paper-pieced log cabin squares. All seams are approximately ⅛" to prevent excess bulk when working with small pieces.

Materials:

Tissue paper

Fabric scraps

Thread

Fray Check

1¼" hinged pin

Thin batting or felt

Assembly:

1. Trace pattern onto tissue paper, being careful to number each strip.

It is necessary to piece a log cabin square for each pin.

2. Select 2 fabrics plus White or Yellow. Cutting requirements for each square.

Make one fabric "A" and one fabric "B" from <u>each</u> fabric. Cut the following strips:

1 - ¾" x ¾" White for center
1 - ¾" x ¾"
1 - ¾" x 1⅜"
1 - ¾" x 1⅝"
1 - ¾" x 2"
1 - ¾" x 2¼"
1 - ¾" x 2¾"

3. Start by centering fabric "A" behind area 1 with the wrong side of the fabric against the untraced side of the pattern. Place it so there is approximately ⅛" seam allowance extending past the line that separates area 1 from area 2.

Continue with the steps listed below until all areas of the pattern are covered with fabric.

4. As you add strips for each step, place them in the right position on the untraced side of the pattern. Flip the strip over, putting right sides together with the strips that are already in place. Use the previously trimmed ⅛" seam allowance. It is best to shorten stitch length for paper piecing.

5. Sew all seams by sewing directly on the lines on the traced side of the pattern. Stitch 1 or 2 stitches before and beyond the ends of the line.

6. It is very important to press each piece to the side after sewing.

7. Fold along the seam line to be sewn next on the untraced side of the pattern.

Tear pattern away if necessary from stitches to allow folding on the line.

Trim away excess fabric, leaving a ⅛" seam allowance along the fold.

8. When log cabin square is completed, tear away tissue pattern.

Layer the square, right side up, with a piece of thin batting or felt and a piece of backing fabric.

9. Quilt the layers together.

10. Copy pattern (bird, heart, star, Texas) . Place desired pattern on the log cabin block.

Topstitch around the pattern ⅛" inside of the outside line.

11. Remove tissue paper pattern and trim ⅛" outside the topstitch line just sewn.

12. If desired, coat raw edges with Fray Check to prevent fraying.

13. Sew a 1¼" hinged pin on back.

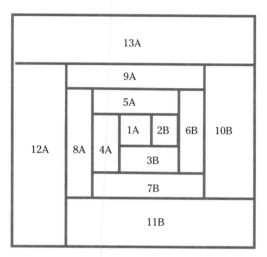

LOG CABIN PATTERN

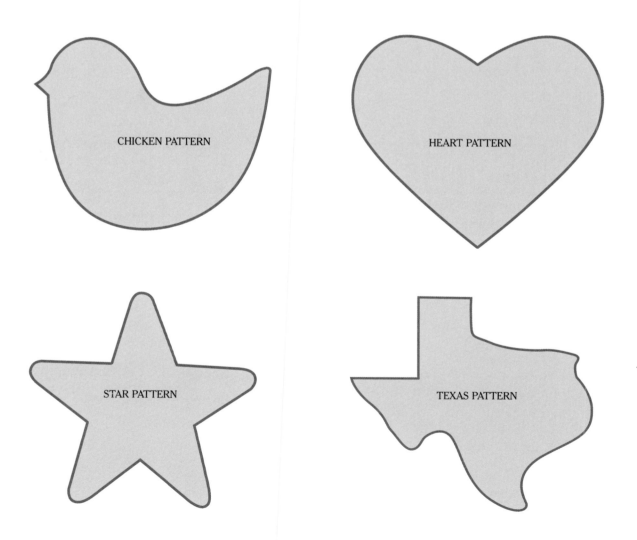

CHICKEN PATTERN

HEART PATTERN

STAR PATTERN

TEXAS PATTERN

Friendship Pins

continued from pages 80 - 81

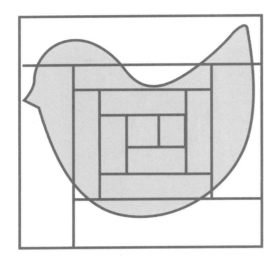

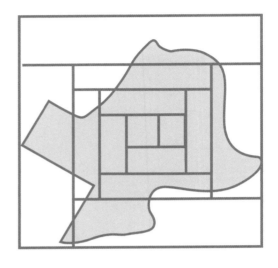

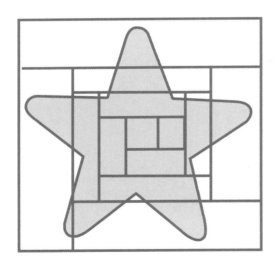

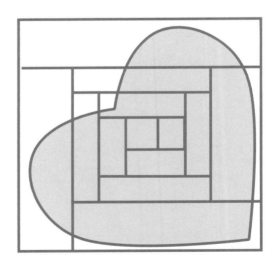

PLACEMENT DIAGRAMS